Table of Contents

Foreword by
Danie Veldsman, PhD

What has pleasantly surprised me in my theological friendship with Kobus over almost twenty years in South Africa and in Canada, is his deep intuitive understanding of at least two characteristics of being a Reformed theologian. He lives in his personal and congregational life the Reformed Latin motto of *ecclesia reformata semper reformanda*. It is, to keep on reforming, to unceasingly be in search of new ways to give expression to our commitment to God in Jesus Christ through his Spirit. It is to find new paths on which we can walk our talk with God and to pave new paths that are a witness to God's gracious love and faithfulness. These paths stretch and run through lives, through churches, but also over continents - paths that are a witness to the one good message of God's love and faithfulness to all of God's creation.

This, Kobus has continuously pursued enthusiastically and adventurously, and his book, *Hearing God's Tweet*, is a witness to his endeavours over the years – a welcoming invitation to the attentive ear, and to the hungry mind!

But a second Reformed characteristic also finds expression (again captured in a Latin phrase) in his publication, namely that of *sola scriptura*, that is, the primary importance of Scripture within the lives of those who confess to belonging to God. In a creative and delightful manner, Kobus breaks open in *Hearing God's Tweet* the bread (God's Word) of concrete life to still the hunger of those who are in search of belonging - of belonging as the answer to the "looking-for-us-by God". Both these Reformed characteristics are methodologically neatly tied together in his book. It is tied together in such a way that I would like to use a third Latin expression – *credo ut intelligam* – [coined by the great

Medieval Italian theologian Anselmus (c. 1033-1109)] to describe the "tied knot" in *Hearing God's Tweet*. It simply means: "Faith seeking understanding".

Kobus has succeeded in this original and creative publication, not only to enrich our faith and to deepen our engagement on the road to understanding, but perhaps also to welcome those who may hear God's loving and graceful *Tweet* for the first time.

- Pretoria, South Africa 2011

Introduction

I think it is fair to say that two thirds of the world is covered with water while the rest is covered with Facebook, and Twitter.

These social network phenomena have captured the imaginations of the world and changed the way people live.

But it is the Twitter phenomenon that has intrigued me – maybe because of its simplicity and the use of the word "tweet." For some reason, that word has grabbed my attention and prompted the birth of this devotional.

Hearing God's Tweet is a daily devotional, which serves as an invitation to follow God and what God is doing.

Each devotion consists of five elements:
1. *The heading* represents God's Tweet.
2. *The Bible passage* relates to God's Tweet.
3. *The devotion* is an application of the passage to our lives.
4. *A short prayer* follows the devotion.
5. *"Today's quote"* relates to the overall message of that specific devotion.

The devotions in Hearing God's Tweet take you on a journey through all the Bible books. The devotions don't follow the order of the Bible books as presented in the Bible but rather the chronological order of events. This will help you to get the bigger picture of the Bible. You can look at the devotions as jigsaw puzzle pieces of the bigger picture of the Bible.

My prayer is that these tweets will help you to be overwhelmed by God's beauty and God's love through Jesus Christ.

All Scripture is God-breathed and is useful for teaching, rebuking, correcting and training in righteousness, so that the servant of God may be thoroughly equipped for every good work.
(2 Timothy 3: 16-17 NIV ©2011)

Beginning - Tweets
(Genesis 1–11)

The events in Genesis 1–11 bear no date and are therefore known as pre-history. The following important events occur during this time:

▶ Creation
Creation is God's proclamation that He wants to accompany human beings on their life journey.

▶ Adam and Eve
Human beings are the highlight of the creation.

▶ Cain and Abel
Human beings disappoint God. Cain murders his brother Abel.

▶ Noah and the Flood
God regrets creating human beings (Gen. 6:6) and decides to use water to destroy them. God shows mercy by saving Noah and his family. After the flood, God makes a promise to never again repeat this event. The rainbow is proof of His promise. Yes, God is with us all the time.

▶ The Tower of Babel
Human beings once again disobey God. They decide to make a name for themselves by building the Tower of Babel.

The first 11 chapters of Genesis describe how human beings miss the mark. The rest of the Bible tells us how God accompanies human beings on their journey through life in order to create a community of believers—a family of faith!

Beginning with something so exciting and amazing! Hard to express it in words!

Bible passage

Genesis 1 *God's creation*

1 In the beginning God created the heavens and the earth. ² Now the earth was formless and empty, darkness was over the surface of the deep, and the Spirit of God was hovering over the waters. *(NIV)*

Devotion

The word "beginning" is a wonderful word because it contains elements of expectation, optimism and excitement. Think of the first day of holiday, the kick-off of a football game, or your first date. It is striking to note that the very first sentence in the Bible contains this word. It is here where our journey begins. Isn't that cool?

The first sentence in the Bible is an announcement that proclaims God is the creator of all. Everything begins with God! *"The Spirit of God was hovering over the waters"* in verse 2 symbolizes God's mysterious presence and power. It is this mysterious power that could equip a stutterer like Moses to lead his people, turn a defenseless widow like Naomi into a joyous grandmother, stop Saul in his tracks, or enable Jesus to rise from the dead. On this Tweet-journey, you will discover how God's Spirit is still alive. You should only learn to see this. In short, this journey begins with God. *You could not have wished for a better start!*

Prayer

Loving Father and Creator of all, I come to you today deeply grateful for your creation. I am amazed at the greatness and majesty of all that You have made. Thank You for letting me know You. I look forward to discovering how Your Spirit works in my life.

Today's Quote

Nobody can go back and start a new beginning, but anyone can start today and make a new ending.
—Maria Robinson

Enjoying My masterpiece and taking a break on the seventh day

The story of creation has given rise to much debate, but the question stands: Does Genesis 1 have a message for us? Let's take a look.

Day	God's actions	Day	God's actions
1	light and time	4	sun, moon and stars
2	sky sea	5	birds (sky) fish (sea)
3	land & plants	6	animals & man

During the first three days God prepares the earth to be inhabited by taming the forces of darkness and barrenness. During the last three days, God completes the cosmos in the same sequence as the first three days: the heavenly bodies (sun, moon and stars) to drive away the darkness; the birds to fill the air and the fish to fill the seas; animals and human beings to live from the land and plants.

This wonderful parallel tells us that God created in an orderly fashion and put everything in place for relationships to flourish. God wants you to experience healthy relationships with Him, with other people and with creation.

Prayer
Indescribable, uncontainable
You placed the stars in the sky
And You know them by name
You are amazing, God
(From the song Indescribable *by Laura Story and Jesse Reeves*)

Today's Quote
*Two things fill the mind with ever new and increasing admiration and awe —
the starry heavens above and the moral law within.*
—Immanuel Kant

Going for a walk and realizing that Adam and Eve are hiding. Calling to them: "Where are you?"

Bible passage

Genesis 3: 1-22 *The Fall of Humankind*

6 When the woman saw that the fruit of the tree was good for food and pleasing to the eye, and also desirable for gaining wisdom, she took some and ate it. She also gave some to her husband, who was with her, and he ate it. [9] But the LORD God called to the man, "Where are you?" *(NIV)*

Devotion

We all want to experience freedom. The reality is that your freedom stops where someone else's freedom starts. That is why houses have doorbells. People need to ask permission to enter your free space. Freedom entails boundaries that need to be respected.

Adam and Eve were not allowed to eat from the fruit of the tree in the middle of the garden. The tree is a symbol of God's presence and therefore indicates that the garden belongs to Him. The tree therefore sets a boundary between God and human beings. We need to respect those boundaries. By choosing to respect the boundaries we are expressing our love and respect to God. Unfortunately Adam and Eve did not respect those boundaries by eating from the forbidden fruit. They realize that and hide from God. Fortunately God does not turn His back on them but calls to them.

No matter what you have done, God will still be looking for you to show you how much He loves you.

Prayer

Lord, forgive me where I didn't show respect and thank You for never turning your back on me.

Today's Quote

Lieutenant Daniel Taylor: "*Have you found Jesus yet, Gump?*"
Forest Gump: "*I didn't know I was supposed to be looking for him, sir.*"
From the movie: Forest Gump Robert Zemeckis, 1994

Heartbroken because of humankind's wickedness! Sorry I ever made people and plan to destroy every living thing

Bible passage

Genesis 6: 5-8 *God is grieved*

7 So the LORD said, 'I will wipe mankind, whom I have created from the face of the earth – men and animals, and creatures that move along the ground, and birds in the air – for I am grieved that I have made them.'
[8] But Noah found favor in the Eyes of the Lord. *(NIV)*

Devotion

Shortly after God created everything good, the Bible tells us of humankind's failure - Adam and Eve ate the forbidden fruit and Cain killed his brother, Abel. Humankind's sins cause God tremendous pain because God loves them. The word "grieved" in this passage literally means that His heart was filled with pain. The same Hebrew word for "grief" is used in Genesis 3:16 to describe the pain women have to endure during childbirth, and in Genesis 3:17 to describe men's toil to earn a living. By deliberately using the same word, the Bible says something remarkable: Our pain has spilled over to God. God is therefore not detached from what happens to us.

Because God is disappointed, God plans to wipe out humankind and even the animals from the face of the earth. But then something impressive happens, as the word "but" in verse 8 indicates:

God changes his mind. God's love for humans is always stronger than His wrath. Isn't that comforting to know – especially when we mess up?

Prayer

Thank you that the will of God will never take me to where the grace of God will not protect me.

Today's Quote

There but for the grace of God go I.
— Author unknown

Realizing that human beings are busy building a tower and deciding to go down to check it out

Bible passage

Genesis 11: 4-8 *The Tower of Babel*
4 'Come, let us build ourselves a city, with a tower that reaches to the heavens, so that we may make a name for ourselves ... *(NIV)*

Devotion

"Live your dream!" "If you can dream it, you can achieve it!" "Reach for the stars!" Ambitious people are inspired by utterances such as these. Ambition is a good thing, but it can be dangerous. The well-known story of the Tower of Babel illustrates the danger of ambition.

In the past, people believed that the gods lived on the mountain tops. Because Mesopotamia (modern-day Iraq), did not have high mountains, people built ziggurats to perform this function. Ziggurats were massive pyramidal temples. It served as meeting places between heaven and earth—between the gods and human beings. The base of a ziggurat could be about 300 square feet and have a height of about 300 feet. The room at the top was used for religious practices.

The story of the Tower of Babel was most probably told with reference to the ziggurats. They were very ambitious. There is nothing wrong with ambition. Unfortunately they use their ambition to compete with God and to exclude God. Ambition should always take God into account, for this will prevent us from becoming **arrogant** and trampling on others. Arrogant people always think they are better than other people. Humble people are easily liked, very approachable and easy to get along with. Be humble and thank God for your accomplishments!

Prayer
Lord, I would like to always take You into account in my ambitions!

Today's Quote
Arrogance diminishes wisdom.
– Arabian proverb

ambition

The Ancestors of the Israelites - Tweets
(±2000 – ± 1250 BC)
(Genesis 12–50)

▶ God calls Abraham
God is grieved because He created human beings (Gen 6:6). Nevertheless, He wants to accompany them on their journey. The means by which He chooses to do this is to single out one man and his family and turn them into a nation that will have a very special relationship with Him.

▶ Isaac is born for Abraham

▶ Jacob is born for Isaac

▶ Jacob, later called Israel, had twelve sons who became the ancestors of the twelve tribes of Israel.

▶ Joseph, one of Jacob's sons, becomes a consultant for the king of Egypt. He invites Jacob's whole family to come and stay in Egypt.

In these chapters in Genesis, we see the wondrous ways God goes about establishing a new community of faith.

Planning to put Abraham's faith to the ultimate test by asking him to sacrifice his only son, Isaac

Bible passage

Genesis 22: 1-19 *Abraham Tested*

13 Abraham looked up and there in a thicket he saw a ram caught by its horns. He went over and took the ram and sacrificed it as a burnt offering instead of his son. [14] So Abraham called that place The LORD Will Provide. *(NIV)*

Devotion

We often encounter times when it seems as if life has reached a dead end and there is no way forward. This episode might help us see the light!

The episode in which Abraham was to sacrifice Isaac must have made Abraham doubt God's logic. How could God ask him to do such a thing? Had not God promised him land and numerous descendents? And now he was to sacrifice his only son. Yet despite his inability to understand, Abraham obeys God. In the end, Abraham sacrifices a ram, not Isaac. Was it a *coincidence* that the ram was there? No, Abraham sees this as a sign that God provides. He calls the place "the Lord will provide." What seemed like a dead end to Abraham was actually a new beginning.

Right now, things may be happening in your life that just do not make sense. May this be an opportunity for you to experience that the Lord will provide a way out.

Prayer

Lord, help me to trust You even though it feels there is no way out.

Today's Quote

The pessimist sees difficulty in every opportunity. The optimist sees the opportunity in every difficulty.
—Winston Churchill

Realizing that the seventeen-year-old Joseph's arrogance will bring him into disrepute with his brothers

Bible passage

Genesis 37: 5-11 *Joseph's Dreams*

5 Joseph had a dream, and when he told it to his brothers, they hated him all the more. *(NIV)*

Devotion

I am pretty sure that you've come across a person who thinks that he/she is always right and who believes that he/she is truly better than other people. This is what we call an arrogant person. Arrogant people are not popular. Joseph was very arrogant when he was a teenager. He had a dream and revealed it to his brothers. The meaning of the dream is very clear: Joseph will become a ruler and his father and brothers will be subservient to him. Joseph's arrogance makes his brothers' blood boil.

That is aggravated by the fact that he is their father's favourite child. That is why, in the next episode, they throw him into an empty cistern and sell him later as a slave. Joseph learns the hard way that arrogance brings you into disrepute. You don't have to learn it the hard way! Just be humble!

Prayer

Lord God, help me to be still and know that You are God. Help me to remember my sins, to confess them to You, and ask Your forgiveness. I pray in the name of Jesus for help in overcoming _____
I realize that arrogance brings us into disrepute. Help me to be humble and to live to your glory! Amen

Today's Quote

Arrogance and rudeness are training wheels on the bicycle of life –
for weak people who cannot keep their balance without them.
— Laura Teresa Marquez

Seeing that Potiphar's wife wants to cheat on her husband by taking handsome Joseph to bed

Bible passage

Genesis 39: 1-23 *Potiphar's wife tries to seduce Joseph*

6 So he left in Joseph's care everything he had; with Joseph in charge, he did not concern himself with anything except the food he ate. Now Joseph was well-built and handsome, [7] and after a while his master's wife took notice of Joseph and said, 'Come to bed with me!' *(NIV)*

Devotion

Everyone faces temptations. A temptation is the desire to have or do something that you know you should avoid. Joseph can help us to deal with temptation. Joseph was Potiphar's (he was the captain of Pharaoh's guard) personal attendant.

Potiphar's wife starts flirting with Joseph. She makes attempts to seduce him into sleeping with her. After all, Joseph is muscular and well built. Joseph resists the temptation by running away from it.

Temptations normally start with a harmless thought. Then you start to entertain that thought. Then you commit the act. Joseph didn't entertain the temptation.

I know it is not always easy. Maybe you are in the grip of something you know is harmful. Talk to someone you can trust! No one is perfect! We all make mistakes!

Prayer

Dear Lord, You know the temptations that I am facing today. I ask for your strength to stand up under the temptation whenever I encounter it. Please, Lord, give me the wisdom to walk away when I am tempted, and the clarity to see the way out that you will provide. I pray this in Jesus' name. Amen

Today's Quote

It is easier to stay out than get out.
— Mark Twain

Heart going out to Joseph who is treated unfairly and thrown into prison

Bible passage

Genesis 40: 6-23 *Joseph interprets the cupbearer's dream*
12 'This is what it means,' Joseph said to him. 'The three branches are three days. ¹³ Within three days Pharaoh will lift up your head and restore you to your position and you will put Pharaoh's cup in his hand, just as you used to do when you were his cupbearer. *(NIV)*

Devotion

I will never forget my first psychology class at university for what the professor said. He said that life is unfair. Isn't that true? Joseph experienced that when he was thrown into prison for supposedly raping Potiphar's wife. Potiphar's wife lied because she was mad that Joseph didn't want to sleep with her. Although he did nothing to deserve it, he was made a slave and prisoner for 13 years. Fortunately, the story does not end there.

In prison he meets Pharaoh's cupbearer and chief baker. They were thrown in prison for offending Pharaoh. They both had dreams and Joseph was able to interpret the dreams for them. Two years later Joseph was released from prison because he was able to interpret Pharaoh's dream. We learn from Joseph that we mustn't become bitter when life is unfair but to continue to trust God. I know it is not always easy but Romans 8 verse 28 is always a comfort: "*And we know that in all things God works for the good of those who love him, who have been called according to his purpose.*"

Prayer

Lord, thank You that I can know that despite my circumstances, You are constantly working in my life.

Today's Quote

Out of difficulties grow miracles.
—Jean de la Bruyere

Revealing the meaning of Pharaoh's dreams to Joseph

Bible passage

Genesis 41: 8-41 *Pharaoh's Dreams*

8 In the morning his mind was troubled, so he sent for all the magicians and wise men of Egypt. Pharaoh told them his dreams, but no one could interpret them for him.

[16] "I cannot do it," Joseph replied to Pharaoh, "but God will give Pharaoh the answer he desires." *(NIV)*

Devotion

We sometimes feel the absence of God in our lives. The episode where Joseph interprets Pharaoh's dream will help us to deal with this feeling.

Pharaoh's magicians couldn't tell Pharaoh the meaning of his dream. Joseph is brought from prison to the mighty Pharaoh's palace to interpret Pharaoh's dream. The Pharaoh is so impressed with Joseph's interpretation that he makes him second in command in the whole land of Egypt. Joseph progresses from a prison to a palace — without pertinent mention of God (except in Genesis 45:5–8 and 50:19–20). Wow!!

Was God absent? Certainly not! God often achieves His goal by using ordinary people and ordinary events. Trust God even when you don't feel His presence.

Prayer

Thank You, Lord, for letting me know that You are constantly working in my life.

Today's Quote

Small minds are concerned with the extraordinary, great minds with the ordinary.

—Blaise Pascal

From Slavery in Egypt to the Conquest of the Promised Land - Tweets

(±1250 – ± 1220 BC)

(Exodus, Leviticus, Numbers, Deuteronomy and Joshua)

▶ The ancestors of Israel become slaves for almost 450 years in Egypt

▶ God renews his covenant with Abraham when He calls Moses to lead the Israelites from Egypt.

   - The ten plagues

▶ The Israelites wander for forty years in the desert.

   God makes a covenant with the people at Mount Sinai.

   A constitution is formed for God's new people.

   God gave Moses the Ten Commandments (Exod. 20).

   The sad episode of the golden calf

   Fire and cloud columns lead the people.

   The Tabernacle is built.

   God sends provision of manna and quails.

▶ Invasion of Canaan, the Promised Land

We now see that God is starting to fulfill His promises made to Abraham.

Unfortunate that Pharaoh thinks he will get away with his sick plan

Bible passage

Exodus 2: 1-10 *Moses' birth*

9 Pharaoh's daughter said to her, 'Take this baby and nurse him for me, and I will pay you.' So the woman took the baby and nursed him. [10] When the child grew older, she took him to Pharaoh's daughter and he became her son. She named him Moses, saying, "I drew him out of the water." *(NIV)*

Devotion

Can I trust God with my problems? The episode where Pharaoh orders that new-born Hebrew babies be thrown into the Nile will give us some wisdom. In this episode, we see that women, who at that time had no real power, jeopardize the mighty Pharaoh's plans. This starts with Moses' mother, who hides her son, Moses, in the reeds while Moses' sister stands at a distance. Pharaoh's own daughter then comes to Moses' rescue. However, she does not want to take responsibility for his upbringing, so, without realizing it, she returns him to his own mother, who feeds him and takes care of him.

The best part is that the princess pays Moses' mother to do this! God uses socially disempowered women to undermine the mighty Pharaoh's plans. Unbelievable! God is still able to provide a way out in surprising and unpredictable ways. Trust God with your challenges!

Prayer

Thank You, Lord, for letting me know that You are in control of history.

Today's Quote

Love is like an earthquake - unpredictable, a little scary, but when the hard part is over you realize how lucky you truly are.

— Anonymous

Hearing the cry of the Israelites in the desert and deciding to provide for their needs

Bible passage

Exodus 16 *The LORD Sends Food from Heaven*
11 The LORD said to Moses, [12] "I have heard the grumbling of the Israelites. Tell them, 'At twilight you will eat meat, and in the morning you will be filled with bread. Then you will know that I am the LORD your God.' " *(NIV)*

Devotion

I sometimes wonder if God really cares, and if God is aware of my suffering. The good news is that it echoes on many occasions in the Bible that God hears our cry. In this episode, God hears the cry of His people who are suffering greatly in the desert. Their desert experience was aggravated by the shortage of water and food. The desert was also extremely hot and filled with uncertainties. God doesn't only hear their cry but also provides for their need for meat (quail at night) and bread (manna during the day). God uses their desert experience to teach them to trust Him. Your own desert experience may be the Lord's way to teach you to trust Him. Remember, God hears your cry - always!

Prayer

Hear my cry O Lord attend unto my prayer
From the end of the earth will I cry out to Thee.
when my heart is overwhelmed
Lead me to the Rock that is higher than I
That is higher than I.
(words from the song "Hear my cry, O Lord")

Today's Quote

God whispers to us in our pleasures, speaks in our conscience, but shouts in our pains: it is His megaphone to rouse a deaf world.
—C.S. Lewis

Meeting with Moses on Mount Sinai to give him the Ten Commandments as the rule of life

Bible passage

Exodus 20 *The Ten Commandments*

3 "You must not have any other god but me.

12 "Honor your father and mother.

13 "You must not murder. *(NIV)*

Devotion

We don't always like rules. We feel that it restricts us and spoils our fun. Is that the case with the Ten Commandments? No! The Ten Commandments are to us what water is to a fish and tracks to a train. A fish is only free in water as is a train on tracks. We are only free within the boundaries of the Ten Commandments.

Freedom therefore always entails boundaries. The boundaries of the Ten Commandments are not our restriction but our freedom to build healthy relationships with God and people.

The first four commandments tell us how to love God while the last six commandments tell us how to love people.

The Ten Commandments help us to become the people God wants us to be. The famous Dutch theologian, A.A. van Ruler, makes a striking observation by saying that the Lord did not create us in the Old Testament so that he could turn us into Christians in the New Testament. According to van Ruler, the Lord makes Christians of us in the New Testament so that we can become human beings again—human beings in the way God intended us to be. You are free to love!

Prayer

Lord, thank you for the freedom I can experience by following the Ten Commandments.

Today's Quote

Preach the gospel at all times, and when necessary use words.
—Saint Francis of Assisi

Furious at the Israelites for making the golden calf

Bible passage

Exodus 32 *The Israelites worship a golden calf*

7 The LORD said to Moses: Hurry back down! Those people you led out of Egypt are acting like fools. [8] They have already stopped obeying me and have made themselves an idol in the shape of a young bull. They have bowed down to it, offered sacrifices, and said that it is the god who brought them out of Egypt.

[14] So even though the LORD had threatened to destroy the people, he changed his mind and let them live. *(NIV)*

Devotion

As Moses is experiencing a spiritual high on top of the mountain in the presence of God, the people are experiencing a spiritual low at the foot of the mountain. Because Moses stayed away for such a long time, they begin to believe that Moses has failed them. So, they decide to make a golden calf to lead them into the desert.

God was so angry that He decided to destroy them. How on earth could they dare to replace God with a calf? Moses tried to talk God out of it. The good news is that God changed His mind and forgave them.

One of the most liberating thoughts must be to know that God can change His mind because His love always supersedes His anger. Thank God that He deals with us not out of anger but out of compassionate love!

Prayer

Thank You, Lord, that You can change Your plans because of Your wonderful mercy!

Today's Quote

I have always found that mercy bears richer fruits than strict justice.
— Abraham Lincoln

Giving instructions to Moses to ordain Aaron as high priest and his sons as priests

Bible passage

Leviticus 8: 1-30 *Ordination of priests*

30 Next Moses took some of the anointing oil and some of the blood that was on the altar, and he sprinkled them on Aaron and his garments and on his sons and their garments. *(NLT)*

Devotion

At times, we might feel that we are of no real use because we have so often failed God and our fellow human beings. The ordination of Aaron as high priest and of his sons as priests will help us to see this differently.

A high priest had to perform very important duties at the Tabernacle. One would think that God would appoint an exceptional person to this position. Instead, God appointed someone with a less favourable record — Aaron. Aaron was the one who had made the golden calf while Moses met with God on Mount Sinai.

Aaron's sins drove God close to destroying His people. Yet, despite this incident, Aaron was ordained as high priest. From this, we see that God is able to use anyone - even you!

Prayer

Thank You, God that You want to use me. Thank You that I no longer have to feel useless. Use me!

Today's Quote

Choose the life that is most useful, and habit will make it the most agreeable.
— Francis Bacon

you are useful

Talking to Aaron after the tragic death of his two sons about respecting God

Bible passage
Leviticus 8: 1-30 *Ordination of priests*
30 Then Moses took some of the anointing oil and some of the blood from the altar and sprinkled them on Aaron and his garments and on his sons and their garments. So he consecrated Aaron and his garments and his sons and their garments. *(NIV)*

Devotion
God wants us to respect Him. Aaron's two sons died because they didn't show respect to God. It reminds me of a fellow student of mine, who often would interrupt a respected professor during lectures by asking him questions, some of which were quite irritating. Once my friend confronted the professor with the following question: "Professor, if the Lord is my friend, can I walk around on campus and talk to God and tell God that there is nothing like a pair of pretty legs?" A dead silence fell over the lecture room, because this young man had once again dared to frustrate the distinguished professor. The professor answered with a loving, yet stern, expression: "Young man, the Lord is your friend but not your buddy."

Prayer
God, heaven and earth are full of your glory. Your love is great enough to embrace the universe. Lord, forgive me for not always showing You the necessary respect.

Today's Quote
A true love of God must begin with a delight in his holiness.
– Jonathan Edwards

Asking Moses to give the Israelites instructions in how to be holy

Bible passage

Leviticus 19 *Moses talks to the Israelites*

1 The Lord also said to Moses, [2] "Give the following instructions to the entire community of Israel. You must be holy because I, the Lord your God, am holy. *(NIV)*

Devotion

What does it mean to be holy? Unfortunately the word "holy" is associated with being stuck up ("holier than thou"). Popularly we may suppose that "holy" means "morally good". The core meaning of holiness is not "good" but rather "set apart" - and therefore, good. To be "set apart" means that something or someone is different. This theme is of such importance in the book of Leviticus that the word "holy" is used 152 times. God wanted the Israelites to lead a holy life, because this would serve as a testimony to other nations that God is holy and therefore different from other gods. A holy life also makes it easier for others to believe, because they witness something different. What does your life reflect? Ask someone today if they know what "holy" means.

Prayer

Dear Jesus, help me to spread your fragrance everywhere.

Flood my soul with your Spirit and life.

Penetrate and possess my whole being so utterly that all my life may be only a radiance of yours.

Shine through me and be so in me that every person I come in contact with may feel your Presence in my soul.

Let them look up and see no longer me but only Jesus.

John Henry Newman

Today's Quote

Holiness is doing God's will with a smile.

—Mother Teresa of Calcutta

holiness

Meeting with Moses to share with him what it takes to be a Nazirite

Bible passage

Numbers 6 *Prescriptions for a Nazirite*
1 The LORD said to Moses, [2] 'Speak to the Israelites and say to them: 'If a man or woman wants to make a special vow, a vow of separation to the LORD as a Nazirite, [3] he must abstain from wine and other fermented drink and must not drink vinegar made from wine or from other fermented drink. He must not drink grape juice or eat grapes or raisins. *(NIV)*

Devotion

What is the one characteristic that people admire most in others? That characteristic is commitment. Maybe it is because most people struggle to attain it. People with this characteristic serve as a source of inspiration.

In the time of the Old Testament Nazarites fulfilled the role to inspire. A Nazirite was someone who made a vow to be fully committed to the Lord. A Nazirite vow was not an easy one. It demanded that the person abstain from certain things that played an important role in the lives of the heathen and unbelievers.

It is important to associate with dedicated people. Their inspiration leads us to also become sources of inspiration and hope! Who inspires you?

Prayer

Lord, I would like to be a symbol of devotion to those around me. God, I realize anew the importance of surrounding myself with dedicated people.

Today's Quote

People often say that motivation doesn't last. Well, neither does bathing – that's why we recommend it daily.
– Zig Ziglar

Angry at Aaron and Miriam for being jealous of Moses

Bible passage

Numbers 12 *Miriam and Aaron are jealous of Moses*

1 Miriam and Aaron began to talk against Moses because of his Cushite wife, for he had married a Cushite. 2 "Has the LORD spoken only through Moses?" they asked. "Hasn't he also spoken through us?" And the LORD heard this. *(NIV)*

Devotion

We all long for healthy, long-term relationships. However, in our search to form relationships and maintain them, we often fail because of a certain "cancer" that we do not always take into account. What could this cancer be? Jealousy is the cancer in relationships.

Jealousy causes people to be restless — to feel dissatisfied with their own lives and use criticism to trample on those around them. Many people like to hear that others have also failed, because this puts them all in the same boat. Jealousy wishes no one joy.

Aaron and his sister, Miriam, were very jealous of their brother, Moses. The reason for their jealousy was Moses' special position in Israel. He did not find their criticism threatening. When Miriam later contracted leprosy because of her criticism, Moses did not take delight in it. On the contrary, he prayed for his sister's recovery. Moses learned to use good to conquer evil. He left behind a good testimonial: "Now Moses was a very humble man, more humble than anyone else on the face of the earth" (Num 12:3).

Prayer

Lord, help me not to be jealous but to be humble instead.

Today's Quote

To cure jealousy is to see it for what it is, a dissatisfaction with self.
—Joan Didion

Instructing Moses to send out men to explore Canaan, the land I promised to them

Bible passage

Numbers 13 *The spies explore the promised land*

30 Then Caleb silenced the people before Moses and said, 'We should go up and take possession of the land, for we can certainly do it.' [31] But the men who had gone up with him said, 'We can't attack those people; they are stronger than we are.' *(NIV)*

Devotion

Love can blind us to the faults of others. However, love is not the only thing that can do this. Fear also has the ability to blind. The 12 spies who explored the Promised Land to see what it had to offer drew different conclusions in their report to Moses of what they had seen. Ten of the 12 came to the following conclusion: "We can't attack those people; they are stronger than we are" (v. 31), while only two (Joshua and Caleb) said, "we can certainly do it" (v. 30). The reason for the radically different report was because of fear. The majority of the spies were scared of the big cities surrounded by thick walls and the gigantic people. Fear blinded them to God's promise that He would give them the land to live in. Fear can paralyze and trap you, especially in the face of tragedy, uncertainty and circumstances beyond your control. What are your fears?

Prayer

Dear Lord, my fear has trapped and consumed me. But I am tired of living under the weight of my fears. Please give me your love and your power to replace these fears. Your perfect love casts out my fear. I thank you for promising to give me the peace that only you can give. I receive that peace now as I ask you to still my troubled heart. Because you are with me, I don't have to be afraid. Amen

Today's Quote

Worry gives a small thing a big shadow.
—Swedish Proverb

Asking Moses to make sure that the offerings are brought at the appointed time

Bible passage

Numbers 28 *The Daily Offerings*

2 "Give these instructions to the people of Israel: The offerings you present as special gifts are a pleasing aroma to me; *(NIV)*

Devotion

God loves us and longs for a relationship with us. The unfortunate reality is that our wrongdoings (sin) cause a rift in our relationship with God and other people. That is why God hates sin. God cannot turn a blind eye to sin and needs to deal with it. The punishment for sin is death but God doesn't want to punish us with death. That is why God introduced the sacrificial system.

The sacrificial system caused the death of an innocent animal instead of a guilty human. The blood 'covered' the sin of the sinner and therefore it could not take away sin permanently. The sacrificial system prophetically pointed to Jesus, who was to come and take away the sins of the world as the ultimate, perfect and final sacrifice for all time and for all humankind.

And so it's no wonder that when John the Baptist, a Jewish prophet, first set his eyes on Jesus, he made a statement that no Jewish person would have missed. "Look, the Lamb of God, who takes away the sin of the world!" (John 1:29 *TNIV*).

Jesus' sacrifice echoes God's love and forgiveness. May our life be an answer to that echo!

Prayer

Lord Jesus Christ, thank you for Your final and perfect sacrifice on the cross. Purify my heart and mind today.

Today's Quote

He's no fool who gives up what he cannot keep to gain what he cannot lose.

—Jim Elliot

Telling Moses that he will not fulfill his dream of entering the Promised Land

Bible passage
Deuteronomy 3: 21-29 *Moses Forbidden to Cross the Jordan*
25 Let me go over and see the good land beyond the Jordan — that fine hill country and Lebanon.' ²⁶ But because of you the LORD was angry with me and would not listen to me. "That is enough," the LORD said. "Do not speak to me anymore about this matter." *(NIV)*

Devotion
It hurts me (and definitely hurts God) when someone calls another person a loser. Maybe you feel like a loser for not reaching your goals (or the goals others have set for you). This can make you lonely and put more pressure on you to perform. Moses could have felt the same. He was the one who led the Israelites out of Egypt and now God is telling him that he will not enter the Promised Land because he had previously disobeyed God (Numbers 2:12). Despite this, Moses was awarded the following titles: "Man of God" (Ezra 3:2), "God's chosen one "(Ps. 106:23), "God's friend "(Exod. 33:11). With titles such as these, nobody could call Moses a failure.

Someone once also said bad things about me. My friend encouraged me when he said: What people say about you doesn't reflect who you are but it reflects who they are. Be strong!

Prayer
God, thank you that I am not a loser. God, help us to realize that the greatest lesson we, and especially our kids, can learn is that we *do* fail, but it's not the end. All we have to do is try, try again.
Help us to understand that defeats and detours can take us to the best places. I thank You for this important lesson.

Today's Quote
Failure is a detour, not a dead-end street.
— Zig Ziglar

Meeting again with Moses to ask him to read the Ten Commandments to the Israelites before they enter the Promised Land

Bible passage

Deuteronomy 5: 1-21 *The Ten Commandments Repeated*

1 Moses summoned all Israel and said: Hear, O Israel, the decrees and laws I declare in your hearing today. Learn them and be sure to follow them. [7] You shall have no other gods before Me.
[18] "You shall not commit adultery. *(NIV)*

Devotion

We all look for happiness, but we often stumble in our quest to obtain it. How can one be truly happy? There are many answers to this question, but one thing is clear: True happiness is only possible within the confines of loving relationships.

Moses realized that there was only one way in which the Israelites would be happy in the Promised Land: if they, again, committed themselves to the Ten Commandments. The reason for this was because all the commandments concerned building healthy relationships. The first four commandments concern our relationship with God, while the last six concern our relationship with other people. These guidelines are our freedom, not our constraint. In the same way that a fish is only free in water, a human being is only free within God's 10 guidelines.

It may be nice to have the latest BlackBerry, iPhone or iPod Touch, but in the end you only find happiness in healthy relationships. How are your relationships?

Prayer

Thank you, God, that I can be truly free and happy by living according to Your commandments.

Today's Quote

The Ten Commandments are not multiple choice.
—Anonymous

Listening how Moses explains to the Israelites the key of life

Bible passage

Duteronomy 30: 15-20 *Choices*

19 "Today I have given you the choice between life and death, between blessings and curses. Now I call on heaven and earth to witness the choice you make. Oh, that you would choose life, so that you and your descendants might live! [20] You can make this choice by loving the Lord your God, obeying him, and committing yourself firmly to him. *(NLT)*

Devotion

The key of life is that you can make choices. Albert Camus, a French novelist, said that life is the sum of all your choices. Within the first 10 minutes of waking up, we make a number of decisions. For many of us, the most important decision during those 10 minutes is what to wear! (and it drives moms nuts when kids cannot make up their minds). But there is something more important than what to wear.

Moses tells us that the most important decision we need to make everyday is to choose life. We can become so fixated on our dreams (or a boyfriend or girlfriend) and so overwhelmed by our problems that we forget to choose life when we wake up in the morning. But how do I choose life? Verse 20 states very clearly that a choice for life is a choice for loving God. Loving God helps you to realize that life is much more than the brand you wear or the car you drive. God is the giver of life and by loving Him you embrace the life God has in mind for you. God wants the best for you! May tomorrow's first 10 minutes be different!

Prayer

God, thank you that I have the freedom to choose.

Today's Quote

Decision is a risk rooted in the courage of being free.
— Paul Tillich

Watching how two spies scout out the Promised Land and stay the night at a prostitute's house

Bible passage

Joshua 2: 1-15 *Two spies and a prostitute in one room*

1 Then Joshua secretly sent out two spies from the Israelite camp at Acacia Grove. He instructed them, "Scout out the land on the other side of the Jordan River, especially around Jericho." So the two men set out and came to the house of a prostitute named Rahab and stayed there that night. *(NLT)*

Devotion

Mutual trust is the last thing one would expect when two spies and a prostitute end up together. As a prostitute, Rahab was only good enough to be used for the pleasure of others. However, in this instance, she encountered two men who did not lust after her body but instead sought her goodness. She promised to hide them in return for being protected when the Israelites planned to invade Jericho. She experienced kindness during the invasion of Jericho when the Israelites protected her and her family.

It is wondrous that she also experienced God's goodness when she was included in the genealogy of Jesus (Matt. 1:5). Rahab was the mother of Boas who married Ruth. Ruth gave birth to Obed and Obed became the forefather of Jesus.

Rahab is also honoured for her faith (Heb. 11:31) and for her good deeds (Jas. 2:25). Rahab's life changed dramatically because of kindness. Be kind to others and see how people (and you) will change!

Prayer

Lord, I have to confess that I am not always kind toward others.

Today's Quote

Goodness is the only investment which never fails.
—Henry David Thoreau

Asking Joshua to circumcise all men before they enter the Promised Land

Bible passage

Joshua 5 *Circumcision at Gilgal*
9 Then the Lord said to Joshua, "Today I have rolled away the shame of your slavery in Egypt." So that place has been called Gilgal to this day. *(NIV)*

Devotion

What do I do about my sorry past? Unfortunately, it is not always that easy to get rid of a sorry past. We all do things that we are ashamed of and would rather forget. Other people's gossip tends to keep our shameful past alive. But the good news is that God wants to remove the guilt that you may have.

The Israelites who wondered in the desert, also had a shameful past. Their disobedience in the desert earned them a reputation of shame and embarrassment. After the Israelites had traveled in the desert for a period of about 40 years, they were ready to enter the Promised Land. But one thing remained to be done before they could do this: they had to be circumcised. (Circumcision is the removal of some or the entire foreskin from the penis.) Circumcision was the sign that the Israelites belonged to God. The previous generation had been circumcised, but the current generation had neglected this practice during their sojourn in the desert. God had asked Joshua to circumcise the Israelites at Gilgal to mark the end of their life of shame and to give them a fresh start.

Many centuries later, the scene at Gilgal changed to Golgotha when God brought an end to our sins and disgrace. Accept it in faith!

Prayer

Thank you, Jesus, that you died for my shameful past. I am forgiven!

Today's Quote

Forgiveness does not change the past, but it does enlarge the future.
— Paul Boese

Telling Joshua to designate cities of refuge where people can seek asylum

Bible passage

Joshua 20: 1-9 *Cities of refuge*

7 So they set apart Kedesh . . ., Shechem . . ., and Kiriath Arba (that is, Hebron) . . . [8] On the east side of the Jordan of Jericho they designated Bezer . . ., Ramoth . . ., and Golan . . . [9] Any of the Israelites or any alien living among them who killed someone accidentally could flee to these designated cities and not be killed by the avenger of blood prior to standing trial before the assembly. *(NIV)*

Devotion

It is a common practice for people seeking asylum at embassies to be protected from persecution by another authority. This practice is also found in the Bible. God instructed Joshua to identify six cities of refuge where a person who had unintentionally committed a murder could enjoy safety from the acts of revenge by the relatives of the deceased. It is interesting to note that the three cities of refuge west of the Jordan are mentioned from north to south, whereas the cities east of the Jordan are mentioned from south to north. The cities were, therefore, situated in such a way that everyone could reach them within a day. The cities of refuge were under the control of God's servants, the Levites. By doing this, God ensured that His servants could see to it that justice prevailed.

God seeks justice for everyone. We should have the courage of our convictions to act against all forms of injustice and inequality. What kind of justice is needed to make this world a better place?

Prayer

Lord, give me the courage to speak out and to act against injustice.

Today's Quote

Justice is truth in action.
—Benjamin Disraeli

Judges - Tweets
(±1200 – ± 1020 BC)
(Judges and Ruth)

▶ The period of the Judges
This period covers the events between the entry into the Promised Land and the establishment of the monarchy in Israel. During this phase, the tribes were not as closely united as they would later become.

▶ Judges
Before the monarchy was established, the judges (leaders sent by God) rules over the Israelites.

▶ Well-known judges
Othniel, Ehud, Deborah, Gideon, Jephtah and Samson.

▶ Dark time
Whereas the people still worshiped God in the time of Joshua, their faith in Him started to dwindle during this phase. The people began to lead an immoral life and wander off after other gods, and the judges were unable to follow in Joshua's footsteps and turn Israel back to the Lord.

▶ Ruth
The story of Naomi and her daughter-in-law, Ruth, also takes place during the time of the Judges.

My heart aches seeing how a youngster loses it and causing his parents so much pain

Bible passage

Judges 14: 1-5 *Samson wanted to marry a Philistine girl*
3 His father and mother replied, 'Isn't there an acceptable woman among your relatives or among all our people? Must you go to the uncircumcised Philistines to get a wife?' But Samson said to his father, 'Get her for me. She's the right one for me.' *(NIV)*

Devotion

The saying goes, "Small children step on your lap, but bigger children step on your heart." Samson's parents, like many other parents, experienced the pain of a child who lost the way. His parents watched helplessly while their only son went completely off the rails. At his birth, God had promised his parents that he would free the Israelites from the Philistines. Now he chooses to marry a Philistine girl, one of the enemy! It drove his parents nuts. You may feel that your parents are old fashioned and that they don't understand you. Maybe your parents have reason for concern.

I once asked a friend of mine what he thought parents should do if this happened to their children. His answer was, "Weather the storm with them. If you choose differently, you take the risk of losing them along the way." Fortunately, Samson's parents did not leave him but weathered the storm with him.

There are not always clear-cut answers for problems at home. What do you think you can do to make a difference?

Prayer

Lord, I pray that You will give me the strength and forbearance to weather the storms of life.

Today's Quote

Your children need your presence more than your presents.
—Jesse Jackson

Sad to see how revenge is destroying lives

Bible passage

Judges 15 *Samson's Vengeance on the Philistines*
7 Samson said to them, "Since you've acted like this, I won't stop until I get my revenge on you."
⁸ He attacked them viciously and slaughtered many of them. *(NIV)*

Devotion

Why are a lot of action movies and thrillers about getting back at somebody? As people we are "hard wired" with a desire for justice. We don't want evil to succeed but rather want to see it put "down hard." But here's the problem: Revenge and justice are not the same thing. Justice is God making things right in His own time and in His own way. Revenge is when the wronged person takes his or her pain and anger out on the wrongdoer. This is exactly what Samson did when he killed a lot of Philistines to avenge his wife's murder.

A pretty good revenge movie is the 2002 film *The Count of Monte Cristo* (PG-13). It is the story of a wronged man who must decide whether to seek revenge or trust God to bring justice. A priest counsels him with the words from Romans 12: 19 "Vengeance is mine; I will take revenge; I will pay them back," says the Lord."

When people wronged you, it is better to deal with it immediately before it becomes an uncontrollable cycle of violent evil like in Samson's story. You can use different avenues to deal with injustice but never seek revenge. There is only one answer to revenge: Stop it!

Prayer

Lord, help me not to turn my anger into revenge and viciousness.

Today's Quote

Before you embark on a journey of revenge, dig two graves.
—Confucius

Watching how a young person is squandering his life by a reckless lifestyle

Bible passage

Judges 16: 1-21 *Samson and Delilah*

1 One day Samson went to Gaza, where he saw a prostitute. He went in to spend the night with her. *(NIV)*

Devotion

What fuelled the cavalier behaviour of teenagers who are driving too fast, engaging in (unprotected) sex and doing drugs? It has been long assumed that teens know it all and will live for ever. A new study finds that not all teenagers function under the assumption that they know it all and will live forever (source: TIME).

There are many reasons why teens act recklessly. Some feel that they are doomed to die young anyway, while others have negative feelings about the future.

Samson is a good example of someone who lives a reckless life. He slept with prostitutes and gave his parents many sleepless nights. But what is so amazing is that neither his parents nor God turned their backs on Samson. They kept loving him. The reason is that love will never fail you. It always protects, always trusts, always hopes, always perseveres (1 Cor 13: 7, 8). Love has the power to change. It can make one person cry and another person sing. We need to keep on loving!

If you live recklessly, ask yourself; "How does what I do impact my loved ones?"

Prayer

Thank you, God, that You show so much compassion, even when I am reckless.

Today's Quote

Reckless youth makes rueful age.
— Benjamin Franklin

Witnessing how a vulnerable widow faces the painful realities of life

Bible passage

Ruth 1: 1-6 *Hopeless situation*

3 Now Elimelech, Naomi's husband, died, and she was left with her two sons.

⁴ They married Moabite women, one named Orpah and the other Ruth. After they had lived there about ten years, ⁵ both Mahlon and Kilion also died, and Naomi was left without her two sons and her husband. *(NIV)*

Devotion

"Everybody hurts" is a brilliant song by R.E.M. describing the reality of life that everybody hurts sometimes. It is not easy to face our painful realities, and therefore we try to escape from them. But does escape help?

Most teens interviewed after attempting suicide say that they did it because they were trying to escape from a situation that seemed impossible to deal with or to get relief from really bad thoughts or feelings. Doing drugs is another means of escape. But can we find comfort if we do this? Naomi's life story tells us no! Naomi lost her husband and two sons in a foreign land. Her story encourages us to deal with our pain and not try to escape from it.

Prayer

Lord, like Naomi, I also feel vulnerable at times. Help me not to escape my realities but to face them.

Today's Quote

Life is not a problem to be solved, but a reality to be experienced.
—Søren Kierkegaard

Allowing Naomi to blame Me for her bitterness

Bible passage

Ruth 1: 19-22 *Naomi arrives in Bethlehem*
20 'Don't call me Naomi,' she told them. 'Call me Mara, because the Almighty has made my life very bitter. *(NIV)*

Devotion

Guilt is what we feel when we have wronged other people but bitterness is what we feel when others have wronged us. Bitterness is probably one of the most difficult emotions to control. It stems from deep disappointment and robs us of our zest for life. We see this in the life of Naomi whose name means pleasant. She becomes very bitter towards God. She feels that God is to blame for the death of her husband and her two sons. She even asked the people not to call her Naomi but rather Mara, which means bitter.

A bitter person is his or her own worst enemy. It is very difficult to maintain any kind of relationship with a chronically bitter person; and bitterness is a major contributing cause of marital and family problems.

Bitterness will not go away by itself. Once bitterness takes root, it is there until we remove it! The best way to deal with bitterness is to face it like Naomi and talk to someone you can trust. Just do it!

Prayer

Lord, forgive me of my rebelliousness and bitterness that blur my vision.
Please show me the way out of my difficulty!

Today's Quote

Bitterness imprisons life; love releases it.
Bitterness paralyzes life; love empowers it.
Bitterness sours life; love sweetens it.
Bitterness sickens life; love heals it.
Bitterness blinds life; love anoints its eyes.
— Harry Emerson Fosdick

Working merciful coincidences behind the scenes in the lives of Naomi and Ruth

Bible passage

Ruth 2: 1-11 *Boaz is sympathetic towards Ruth*

9 Watch the field where the men are harvesting, and follow along after the girls. I have told the men not to touch you. And whenever you are thirsty, go and get a drink from the water jars the men have filled."

[10] At this, she bowed down with her face to the ground. She exclaimed, "Why have I found such favor in your eyes that you notice me—a foreigner?" *(NIV)*

Devotion

Why do I not always experience the presence of God in my life? If we want to answer this question, we first need to know how God works. The book of Ruth gives us further insight into the way God works in our lives. Nothing sensational happens in the lives of Naomi and Ruth.

A few events happen—things that one would normally call "coincidences." Ruth "coincidentally" goes to the land that belongs to Boaz, who "coincidentally" is Naomi's only relative—and also is very rich. It is also a "coincidence" that he is unmarried and shows interest in Ruth, a woman from a foreign land. It is a "coincidence" that he eventually marries her. What we often contribute to "coincidence," is, in actual fact, God who is working behind the scenes. Maybe we need to call these so called coincidences "merciful coincidences." Do you agree?

Prayer

Thank You, Lord, for accompanying me during the dark times of my life. Help me to see how You mercifully work behind the scenes.

Today's Quote

Coincidence is God's way of staying anonymous.

— Author unknown

So good to see when a vulnerable widow becomes a happy grandmother

Bible passage

Ruth 4: 13-22 *Obed is borne*

13 So Boaz took Ruth into his home, and she became his wife. When he slept with her, the Lord enabled her to become pregnant, and she gave birth to a son.

16 Naomi took the baby and cuddled him to her breast. And she cared for him as if he were her own. *(NLT)*

Devotion

The beginning of Naomi's story is in complete contrast to its end. The story starts when she is a vulnerable widow who has lost her husband and her two sons. She was extremely bitter. By chapter 4, the end of the story, this vulnerable widow becomes a happy grandmother holding a baby in her lap. Her bitterness didn't go away by itself. There were no quick fixes in her life.

What she did was to be honest about her bitterness. She also took the initiative of planning her life and taking control of her situation. God blessed her with a grandson who became part of Jesus' genealogy. God's blessings do not exclude our initiatives. For this reason, we have to leave our comfort zones in order to plan our lives. Take action and do not allow yourself to become a victim of your circumstances. Go for it!

Prayer

God, help me not to become a victim of bitterness.

I realize anew that I need to take action.

I thank You that You will open up new opportunities for me.

Today's Quote

Life is 10% what happens to you and 90% how you react to it.

—Charles R. Swindoll

The Kingdom - Tweets
(± 1020 – 925 BC)
(1-2 Samuel, 1 Kings, 1-2 Chronicles, Job, Psalms, Proverbs, Ecclesiastes and Song of Solomon)

▶ Samuel

Samuel anointed the first two kings, namely Saul and David. Initially, he warned the people that they did not need an earthly king because God was their king (1 Sam. 8:5, 20).

▶ Saul

Saul, the first king, unites the tribes into one nation. Saul became king in ±1020 BC. He had a lot of potential, but he did not have God at heart. He disobeyed God on many occasions.

▶ David

David, the second king, makes Jerusalem his capital. He is one of the great characters in the Old Testament. But David also had a dark side, which the Bible does not hide. David united Israel and led them during the most blessed time in her history.

▶ Solomon

David's son, Solomon, becomes the third king in 965 BC and builds the temple in Jerusalem. The completion of the Temple is a testimony to his reign.

Below the surface, things were deteriorating. Solomon's trust in his military power, his many wives and their idols, and his wealth drove a wedge between himself and God. However, God continued to systematically execute His plan of salvation and His promise to Abraham. God's promise to Abraham manifested in David's line of descent.

Who will show the big mouth giant what a little boy can do?

Bible passage

1 Samuel 17: 31-39 *Saul wants to prevent David from fighting Goliath*
32 "Don't worry about this Philistine," David told Saul. "I'll go fight him!"[33] "Don't be ridiculous!" Saul replied. "There's no way you can fight this Philistine and possibly win! You're only a boy, and he's been a man of war since his youth." *(NLT)*

Devotion

Life's problems so easily overwhelm us. This classic story of Goliath and David should encourage any person facing a problem that seems too big to handle. Goliath is the Philistine warrior, famous for his battle with the young David, the future king of Israel.

Goliath drove fear into the Israelites. He was a giant and nobody in Saul's army thought they had the physical ability to defeat Goliath. David showed up and killed Goliath with a stone from his sling. David's decisive victory over Goliath was impressive. But it was the example he set by his faith and his courage that has inspired people through the ages. While Saul saw an enormous giant, David saw a mere mortal who dared to challenge the living God. Saul was concerned about survival, while David was concerned about God's honor. David's triumph made him an international hero—even today.

What is your giant (big problem) that you need to face? Focus on God and remember that you are not alone. God is with you, and God has given you people whom you can trust. Allow them to help you!

Prayer

God, help me to face the giants in my life and to trust You like David.

Today's Quote

Focus on giants — you stumble.
Focus on God — your giants tumble.
—Max Lucado

Impressed with the kindness David shows to Mephibosheth

Bible passage

2 Samuel 9 *David's Kindness to Mephibosheth*
1 One day David asked, "Is anyone in Saul's family still alive—anyone to whom I can show kindness for Jonathan's sake?"
[13]And Mephibosheth, who was crippled in both feet, lived in Jerusalem and ate regularly at the king's table. *(NLT)*

Devotion

Do you know anyone who uses crutches or a wheelchair? Let me introduce you to Mephibosheth. He was only five years old when his dad (Jonathan) and grandfather (King Saul) died in war.

It was custom in those times for the future king to kill all the possible contenders to the throne. The nurse was afraid that David, the designated king, would kill Mephibosheth. She fled, and in her haste she dropped him and he became crippled. He lived in fear of David.

David only heard about his existence much later. What Mephibosheth did not know, was that David did not want to kill him, but instead wanted to show him favour. He had promised Jonathan (1 Sam. 20) and Saul (1 Sam. 24) that he would not wipe out their descendants. However, David kept his promise and took Mephibosheth into the Royal House. Being disabled does not make one a lesser person! Those of us who are not disabled should learn to be more sensitive toward those who are.

Prayer

Thank You, Lord, that this story helps me to understand that a disabled person is not a lesser person, and that those who are not disabled should be more sensitive toward those who are!

Today's Quote

I thank God for many handicaps, for, through them, I have found myself, my work, and my God.
— Helen Keller

Sad to see that David slept with someone else's wife

Bible passage

2 Samuel 11: 1-5 *David makes Bathsheba pregnant*
5 The woman conceived and sent word to David, saying, 'I am pregnant.'
(NIV)

The words "I am pregnant" can express great joy — and perhaps the answer to prayer! However, these words can also be an expression of dismay and disillusionment if they come as a result of a passionate fling. These three words, "I am pregnant," completely changed the lives of a soldier's wife and David, one of the most popular figures in the Bible.

The stories in the Bible are wonderful because they relate to real life. The story of David and Bathsheba is no exception. This story has stirred people's imagination through the ages. The author uses the "empty spaces" in the story to involve us as readers. Did Bathsheba's husband know what was going on between her and David? Was the adulterous deed rape, or did Bathsheba try to seduce David? Did Bathsheba perhaps exploit the situation in an attempt to become queen? Or Did David fall victim to circumstances? We will never know the answers to these questions for sure, but we do know that David's (and Bathsheba's) fling had an unhappy ending.

David most likely wished that he could turn back the clock when he heard those three words from Bathsheba: "I am pregnant." This episode teaches us that when we make choices, we should always be aware of the consequences — and always prepared to bear them.

Prayer

Lord, help me to make level-headed choices under all circumstances.

Today's Quote

It's choice — not chance — that determines your destiny.
— Jean Nidetch

How can someone dare do this??????

Bible passage
2 Samuel 13: 1-22 *Amnon rapes his own sister*
1 Now David's son Absalom had a beautiful sister named Tamar. And Amnon, her half brother, fell desperately in love with her.
[14] But Amnon wouldn't listen to her, and since he was stronger than she was, he raped her. [15] Then suddenly Amnon's love turned to hate, and he hated her even more than he had loved her. "Get out of here!" he snarled at her. *(NLT)*

Devotion
2 Samuel 12 will put any soap opera in the back seat. In this episode Amnon, King David's son, raped his own sister, Tamar. Absalon, Tamar's brother, told her not to tell anyone (verse 20) and when her dad, King David, heard what had happened, he was angry but did nothing to help his daughter (verse 21). Shame on them! We are not always aware that these events are occurring because people think that they are best a kept secret. I want to be crude and put it bluntly — bull!

Silence breeds more anger and feelings of guilt and reproach. The only way for the emotional wounds of innocent victims to heal, for parents to be brought to book, and for all the Amnons around us to confess, is to break the silence. Life is too precious to keep quiet! Go and speak to someone today! Please!!

Prayer
Lord, please give me the courage to break the silence!

Today's Quote
Silence implies consent.
— Author unknown

Sad to see when a cocky and unteachable young man missed a great opportunity

Bible passage

1 Kings 12: 1-24 *Israel Rebels Against Rehoboam*

13 The king answered the people harshly. Rejecting the advice given him by the elders, [14] he followed the advice of the young men and said, "My father made your yoke heavy; I will make it even heavier. My father scourged you with whips; I will scourge you with scorpions." *(NIV)*

Devotion

After Solomon's death, a delegation from the people went to visit his son Rehoboam to ask him whether he was prepared to relieve their tax burden. After discussing it with his young advisors, he told them bluntly: Stuff you! (vers 14) As a result the kingdom ripped apart. That was so unnecessary. But this cocky and unteachable young man missed a great opportunity for growth – and so destroyed the nation.

Rehoboam did not understand the value of being humble and teachable. It was all about himself. He had no interest in what he could give; his aim was to get maximum. He failed to display generosity. He should have asked: "Do I really love the people that I lead?"

There is a Middle East saying that goes, "When you were born you cried and the world rejoiced. Live your life so that when you die the world cries and you rejoice."

Prayer

Oh Lord, I must admit that it's hard to be humble. Remind me each day to remain humble and teachable. Let me show patience, empathy and love.

Today's Quote
Be a river, not a reservoir
—John C. Maxwell

Love to watch the courage of Elijah

Bible passage

1 Kings 18: 20-40 *Elijah's victory on Mount Carmel*

38 Then the fire of the Lord fell and consumed the burnt-offering, the wood, the stones, and the dust, and even licked up the water that was in the trench. [39] When all the people saw it, they fell on their faces and said, 'The Lord indeed is God; the Lord indeed is God.' *(NRSV)*

Devotion

Some consider Elijah to be the greatest prophet of the Old Testament. That was because of the courage he displayed.

What is courage? Courage is the ability to act regardless of the feelings or potential consequences. Courage is following your intuition when the facts are against it. Courage is saying 'I am sorry' when you are at fault, 'I don't know' when you don't, and 'I love you' despite the hurt, anger or fear.

Courage is not something that comes from flying off the handle in moments of need or in emergencies. Courage is not something that can be handed over to you through lessons either. Courage is a way of life.

Elijah is a wonderful example of someone who had courage muscle. He had a lot of courage to be able to pray for judgment on his own people, to confront a wicked king and then stand before hundreds of false prophets on Mount Carmel and challenge their piety. Each day is an opportunity for us to build our courage muscle. Have you lifted any weights of courage lately?

Prayer

Wait patiently for the Lord.
Be brave and courageous.
Yes, wait patiently for the Lord. (Ps 27: 14 *NLT*)

Today's Quote

Courage is not the absence of fear. It is acting in spite of it.
— Mark Twain

Great to see how the returnees from exile find their place and experience a sense of belonging

Bible passage

1 Chronicles 1 *Genealogy of Adam*

1 The descendants of Adam were Seth, Enosh, [2] Kenan, Mahalalel, Jared, [3] Enoch, Methuselah, Lamech, [4] and Noah. *(NLT)*

Devotion

Why did these genealogical registers thrill the people so much? I have always found the genealogical registers in the Bible utterly boring and senseless until I got to realize that the list of names serves a specific purpose. It is like going to a party and realizing that you do not see a single familiar face. You feel uncomfortable and out of place – until you eventually see a few familiar faces. Genealogies helped the Jews, who had returned from exile, to fit in.

The author wrote to the Jews who had returned to the land of Israel after the exile. They were unsure of where they fit in and felt stripped of their identity. The lists could help a returnee to discover, for example, that he or she was from the lineage of Judah or Simeon. This gave the returned exiles a new identity and a sense of belonging.   A   sense   of belonging is the feeling of being connected and accepted within one's family and community. A sense of belonging is important in healthy human development and combating behavior problems and depression.

These seemingly boring lists should, therefore, fill us with wonder —wonder about God, who really cares for us and wants us to belong!

Prayer

Thank You, Lord, that I can know that I am part of Your genealogy.

Today's Quote

If we have no peace, it is because we have forgotten that we belong to each other.
— Mother Teresa

Like to surprise people in the ordinary things of life

Bible passage

1 Chronicles 11: 4-9 *David Captures Jerusalem*
5 The people of Jebus taunted David, saying, 'You'll never get in here!'
But David captured the fortress of Zion, which is now called the City of
David. *(NLT)*

Devotion

We can so easily be carried away by the exceptional achievements listed
in the Guinness Book of Records. Consequently we often overlook and
underestimate the ordinary things in life. This is a pity, because that is
exactly where God often surprises us with His presence. Several ordinary
events happen in this section. As the anointed king, David did what
kings were entitled to do: to choose a capital city and to rebuild it.

He chooses Jerusalem as his capital city.   David did not foresee that
Jerusalem would later become much bigger than the future capital of the
kingdom of David. To Christians, Jerusalem became the place where Jesus
was crucified and resurrected to give them new life. The importance of the
city was later reflected in the figure of speech "the new Jerusalem."

We should not underestimate the ordinary things in life, because we
never know what their outcome will be.   God is able to surprise you
through the ordinary things that you are doing today.

Prayer

Lord, help me not to underestimate the ordinary things in life! Help me
to do the ordinary things extraordinarily well.

Today's Quote

God never wrought miracles to convince atheism, because His ordinary works
convince it.
— Francis Bacon

Grateful to see that the Queen of Sheba realizes that ordinary things matter

Bible passage

2 Chronicles 9: 1-8 *Visit of the Queen of Sheba*

1 When the queen of Sheba heard of Solomon's fame, she came to Jerusalem to test him with hard questions. She arrived with a large group of attendants and a great caravan of camels loaded with spices, large quantities of gold, and precious jewels. When she met with Solomon, she talked with him about everything she had on her mind. ⁴ She was also amazed at the food on his tables, the organization of his officials and their splendid clothing, the cup-bearers and their robes, and the burnt offerings Solomon made at the Temple of the Lord. *(NLT)*

Devotion

It fascinates me that the general public (especially Americans) is so obsessed with the glitz and glamour of Hollywood? I think Hollywood really makes idols out of people. They are not real. Take Paris Hilton for example. She creates an image that sends many into an awe-like state. But does the fascination of Hollywood really matter? This episode will shed some light on this question.

The Bible tells us of the Queen of Sheba's awe for King Solomon's fame and fortune. What also amazes her is how Solomon does ordinary things, such as clothing and table manners, extraordinary well. It just shows you that ordinary things matter. Does the fascination of Hollywood really matter? I think what really matters is when ordinary people do ordinary things extraordinary well.

Prayer

Lord, I realize once again that it is wise to perform my daily duties in a way that will bear testimony to Your love and mercy.

Today's Quote

Excellence is doing ordinary things extraordinarily well.

—John W. Gardner

Too bad that Rehoboam didn't listen to the advice of the people

Bible passage

2 Chronicles 10 *The Northern Tribes Rebels Against Rehoboam*
8 But he rejected the advice that the older men gave him, and consulted the young men who had grown up with him and now attended him.
15 So the king did not listen to the people, *(NRSV)*

Devotion

King Rehoboam's hunger for power, unreasonable demands, lack of compassion for his people, and bad decision-making split the nation of Israel in two. But probably the root of his problems can be found in 2 Chronicles 10: 15: "So the king did not listen to the people…."

We learn from this episode that hearing is not the same as listening; in other words, receiving sounds is not the same as paying attention to them. The King heard the advice (it reached his ear) but he did not listen (it did not reach his brain).

People hunger to feel significant, appreciated and understood. That can only happen if someone really listens. The unfortunate reality is that in these modern times we are very busy. We have multiple distractions such as cell phones, computers, iPods, iPads and 24/7 television. We are constantly talking and texting. Listening, and true understanding, is where deep levels of trust are born. Google today "how to become a better listener? " I thank God that He always listens.

Prayer

You hear, O LORD, the desire of the afflicted;
you encourage them, and you listen to their cry, (Ps. 10: 17 *NIV*)

Today's Quote

Courage is what it takes to stand up and speak; courage is also what it takes to sit down and listen.
—Winston Churchill

Hezekiah's commitment to please Me fill Me with so much joy

Bible passage

2 Chronicles 31 *Hezekiah's Religious Reforms*
20 Hezekiah did this throughout all Judah; he did what was good and right and faithful before the Lord his God. [21]And every work that he undertook … he did with all his heart; and he prospered. *(NRSV)*

Devotion

Hezekiah was a king of Judah who did much to abolish idolatry from his kingdom. His commitment to God's cause made him a successful king. Our culture is one that does not see commitment as something of importance any more. Just look at the divorce rates.

Ken Blanchard, an American author and management expert, said: *"There is a difference between interest and commitment. When you're interested in something, you do it only when it's convenient. When you're committed to something, you accept no excuses, only results."*

Only through commitment can we become fully human and experience a fulfilled life. Rollo May, an American existential psychologist, said: *"The acorn becomes an oak by means of automatic growth; no commitment is necessary. The kitten similarly becomes a cat on the basis of instinct. Nature and being are identical in creatures like them. But a man or woman becomes fully human only by his or her choices and his or her commitment to them. People attain worth and dignity by the multitude of decisions they make from day by day. These decisions require courage."*

Prayer

God, I thank You, for the commitment of Jesus to go all the way to the cross to die for me. I commit myself to You anew!

Today's Quote

The difference between 'involvement' and 'commitment' is like an eggs and ham breakfast: the chicken was 'involved' - the pig was 'committed.'
— Author unknown

commitment

Don't mind that Job is so brutally honest about his pain and suffering

Bible passage

Job 3 *Job's outburst*

11 "Why wasn't I born dead?
Why didn't I die as I came from the womb?
[26] I have no peace, no quietness.
I have no rest; only trouble comes." *(NLT)*

Devotion

Job's suffering is unbearable. He has lost his family, his wealth and health. Subsequently, he struggles with depression and heartache. Job feels that God has turned His back on him. Job has nothing left to live for. Life's pain and heartache can so easily strip us of our purpose in life. Fortunately, Job made it through this dark period of his life. How did that happen?

Job had a brutal outburst against God and life. Job's outburst against God sounds shocking—shocking because a human being dares to speak with such brutal honesty to his Creator. Looking back, however, we see that these honest outbursts against God helped Job to escape from the depths of his misery. We can follow Job's example by verbalizing and uttering our cries of fear and protest against God. Absolute honesty is an important step away from the dumps of despair.

Prayer

Thank You, Lord, for allowing me to protest against You. Thank You for listening!

Today's Quote

Honesty is the first chapter in the book of wisdom.
— Thomas Jefferson

Always willing to listen to the honest protest of people

Bible passage

Job 13 *Job is protesting*
15 God might kill me,
but I have no other hope.
I am going to argue my case with him. *(NLT)*

Devotion

Sometimes, when we hurt and it feels as if the world has turned against us, bitterness and anger can easily overpower us. This makes us want to protest against God. But are we allowed to do this? Will not God turn his back on us if we protest against Him? Job dares to protest against God. However, he does it in style. He says exactly how he feels without being disrespectful of God or rejecting Him. We may express our cries of protest to God in the finest detail, but this does not mean that we reject Him or that we are disrespectful of God. God welcomes our protest, for by protesting we say, "Lord, I'm struggling to believe. Help me to believe again!"

The good news is that we do not sigh alone: "And the Holy Spirit helps us in our weakness. For example, we don't know what God wants us to pray for. But the Holy Spirit prays for us with groanings that cannot be expressed in words" (Rom. 8:26, *NLT*). God is always willing and ready to listen.

Prayer

Thank You, Lord, that I may feel free to voice my protest against You. It is wonderful to know that Your Spirit supports me in this.

Today's Quote

I have not lost faith in God. I have moments of anger and protest.
Sometimes I've been closer to him for that reason.
—Elie Wiesel

Sad to see when a friend is not giving good advice

Bible passage

Job 16 *Job unsatisfied with his friends' advice.*

2 "I have heard all this before.

What miserable comforters you are!

3 Won't you ever stop blowing hot air?

What makes you keep on talking?

4 I could say the same things if you were in my place.

I could spout off criticism and shake my head at you.

5 But if it were me, I would encourage you.

I would try to take away your grief. *(NLT)*

Devotion

Job's friends reached out to him but they didn't always give him good advice. He was actually mad at them. Job needed encouragement, but what he got instead was condemnation.

Here are some practical hints that will help you to be a good friend to someone in need:

1. Ask yourself how you would feel if you were in that person's shoes.

2. Be there to listen, and keep on listening with an attitude of, "I want to understand what you are saying — feel free to talk or to cry."

3. Avoid talkativeness. People want your ear more than your mouth.

4. Show consistent interest. It shows that you really care.

5. Be very sensitive. We are fragile and need to be handled with care.

6. Be sincere. Don't say you understand because many times we don't. All the best!

Prayer

Lord, help me to be a good friend to others who are experiencing heartache and pain.

Today's Quote

Friendship is love with understanding.

— Author unknown

So glad that Job has found peace again

Bible passage

Job 42 *Job responds to the Lord*
5 I had only heard about you before,
but now I have seen you with my own eyes.
⁶ I take back everything I said,
and I sit in dust and ashes to show my repentance." *(NLT)*

Devotion

Many questions about life can drive us crazy—questions such as, "Why did this happen to me?" or "Couldn't God have intervened?" The book of Job teaches us that we cannot capture the greatness of God in all His glory. Previously, Job reacted to God as if he knew exactly what life entailed, but now he realizes that he was arrogant in trying to compete with God on an equal footing. Verse 6 shows Job's intense remorse. The insignificant Job is overwhelmed by God's greatness when he says, "I sit in dust and ashes to show my repentance."

Job does not get clear answers, but he realizes that God is greater than his questions. Our questions about life are often questions about God Himself. Job is not disappointed in this, because his dream in life, to see God (Job 19:27), comes true (v. 5). To "see" God in this case means to meet Him. Job's meeting with God enables him to accept his situation. Instead of finding answers, he finds God.

Prayer

Lord, help me to realize, like Job, that I will not find the answers to all of life's questions. Help me to accept my situation, because You are greater than all my questions.

Today's Quote

Young man, young man, your arm's too short to box with God.
—James Weldon Johnson

Want people to be happy but sad to see how many people squander their life

Bible passage

Psalm 1 *The way to happiness*
1 God blesses those people
who refuse evil advice
and won't follow sinners
or join in sneering at God.
[2] Instead, the Law of the LORD
makes them happy,
and they think about it
day and night. *(CEV)*

Devotion

If there's one thing everyone in the world wants, it's to be happy, to feel like life is good. So why does it seem so hard to find real happiness?

My friend once told me that we couldn't aspire to happiness. His statement didn't make sense to me because we all aspire to happiness. He then said that happiness is rather a by-product of doing what is right. This is exactly what Psalm 1 says.

Successful marketing, however, sells with promises of happiness. It is all about a famous pretty girl or boy, a luxurious car and sex...the ultimate symbols of human happiness. If that is true, Hollywood must be the happiest place on earth. The tabloids portray a different picture of so many stars in pursuit of happiness. Happiness is rather the result of doing what is pleasing to God. Do you agree?

Prayer

Lord, help me to please You with my lifestyle and to realize that happiness will then follow.

Today's Quote

Happiness is not a goal; it is a by-product.
— Eleanor Roosevelt

Good to see that someone is willing to deal with guilt and unfinished business

Bible passage

Psalm 51 *A prayer for forgiveness*
1 Have mercy on me, O God,
because of your unfailing love.
Because of your great compassion,
blot out the stain of my sins.
² Wash me clean from my guilt.
Purify me from my sin.
³ For I recognize my rebellion;
it haunts me day and night. *(NLT)*

Devotion

Not all of us find it easy to open our hearts to others. Sharing our hurt and shame with other people makes us very vulnerable, and once we have done this, we will have no control over what others will do with the information. People often disappoint us because they tell others about something we told them in confidence, which is precisely why we are hesitant to talk to others. But we cannot keep quiet and bottle up our feelings all the time. It is not good for our health.

Fortunately, there is someone we can trust! Tell God exactly what is on your heart. This is where the author of this Psalm started. It will also be helpful if you can share those thoughts with someone you trust. You will feel so much better.

Prayer

Thank You, Lord, that I can open my heart to You.
Let Your Spirit help me to listen to the sorrows of others.

Today's Quote

We're never so vulnerable than when we trust someone – but paradoxically, if we cannot trust, neither can we find love or joy.

— Walter Anderson

So happy when people are using prayer as a vehicle to express their feelings

Bible passage

Psalm 73 *God is good*

14 I get nothing but trouble all day long;

every morning brings me pain.

[17] Then I went into your sanctuary,

O God, and I finally understood the destiny of the wicked. *(NLT)*

Devotion

This poet did not look forward to getting up in the mornings. Life was just too terrible to face. Perhaps he lay awake at night because he could not take his mind off his suffering. His thoughts were preoccupied because he felt that his faith did not benefit him. He just could not understand why he, as a believer, had to suffer the way he did.

Then, in verse 17, we read about the turning point in his life. He stopped trying to understand why he was suffering and decided to start praying. By using prayer as a vehicle to express his feelings, he gained perspective about life. He realized that the ways of the ungodly were not worth his while, as their lives ended in tragedy. He shifted his focus from the prosperity of the ungodly to his relationship with God. This is why, at the end of his struggle, he could confess that it was good for him to be near God. This insight and confession helped him to move forward with his life. The valuable experience of God's presence is often all that we need.

Prayer

Thank You, Lord, that I can reveal my feelings and struggles to You in prayer, and that Your valuable presence is a source of strength to me.

Today's Quote

When you turn to God, you discover He has been facing you all the time.

—Zig Ziglar

Hoping more people will realize that I am a compassionate God who easily forgives

Bible passage

Psalm 103 *God's wonderful love*
8 The Lord is compassionate and merciful,
slow to get angry and filled with unfailing love. *(NLT)*

Devotion

People can be so mean to each other and hurt each other by raking up things that happened in the past. Fortunately, God acts differently. When God is part of our lives, He is not concerned about our previous wrongdoings, nor does He hold it against us. In other words, God does not act in the same way that people would. People would easily say, "Watch out for that person. He/she has a bad past." Instead, God looks at us, who are saved, without holding what we did in the past against us. He does not even think about our past sins, because He has forgotten them. Verses 11-12 use two wonderful figures of speech to support this thought.

God's total forgiveness and removal of our sins is like the distance between heaven and earth and between east and west—they will never meet. Therefore, we need not worry about the sins that we have confessed. People may be cruel and keep on reminding us of them (and may even hold them against us), but not God. May the Lord help us to forgive others to such an extent that we will never use their sins and shortcomings against them, especially during an argument.

Prayer

Thank You, God, for completely forgiving my sins and even forgetting them. I want to praise You for enabling me to free myself from my past. Help me to forgive others.

Today's Quote

We pardon to the extent that we love.
—François de La Rochefoucauld

forgiveness

If more people will have wisdom as their companion on their life's journey

Bible passage

Proverbs 4 *Wisdom is supreme*
5 Get wisdom;
develop good judgment.
⁶ Don't turn your back on wisdom, for she will protect you.
Love her, and she will guard you. *(NLT)*

Devotion

People so easily let us down. There is one companion in life that will never let you down and that is wisdom. In the Biblical sense, wisdom is the ability to judge correctly and to follow the best course of action, based on knowledge and understanding.

Wisdom teaches us to act correctly from the outset so that we need not make mistakes. In this passage, we read about a father who encourages his son to make wisdom his companion on life's journey. His father knows that wisdom will never let him down, for it will always be there to protect and keep him safe (v. 6). Wisdom will help you to be cautious about with whom you share something confidential. It will enable you to think before you act and not be hasty in your actions.

Who can teach you about this wisdom? It might be a good book, a friend or your parents. Regardless, do not wait another moment to make wisdom your companion.

Prayer

God, help me to act wisely in order to avoid getting hurt unnecessarily.

Today's Quote

The next best thing to being wise oneself is to live in a circle of those who are.
—C.S. Lewis

Wonder if people know what their most precious possession should be?

Bible passage

Proverbs 22 *The value of a good reputation*
1 Choose a good reputation over great riches;
being held in high esteem is better than silver or gold. *(NLT)*

Devotion

Your most precious possession is not your house, smart phone or car. Your most precious possession is your good reputation. Once you have lost it, it so hard to get it back.

There is nothing wrong with being rich and having nice possessions. Unfortunately, money has become an obsession to many people.

The sad part is that many people often neglect other important things in their pursuit of wealth, and then have regrets later on. Many parents realize, too late, that they did not spend enough time with their children. This is often the cause of bad feelings (v. 1) and broken relationships in families. I once read something that had a great impact on me: "Success at work can never make up for failure at home." Children do not only need their parents' money but also their time and love.

Our good name is our most precious possession. Look after it! If we live wisely, we need not worry about what people think of us.

Prayer

Lord, help me to always remember that my good name is more precious than great riches.

Today's Quote

*The legacy of heroes is the memory of a great name
and the inheritance of a great example.*
—Benjamin Disraeli

precious

Wish people would stop comparing themselves with others

Bible passage

Proverbs 31: 10-31 *In praise of a good wife*
28 Her children stand and bless her.
Her husband praises her:
[30] Charm is deceptive,
and beauty does not last;
but a woman who fears the Lord
will be greatly praised. *(NLT)*

Devotion

Why are most people, especially teens, unhappy with the way they look? Maybe their dissatisfaction is linked to Jessica Simpson in her Daisy Duke cutoffs, Paris Hilton and her bikini commercial or sexy Brad Pitt on the latest front cover. Maybe this unhappiness goes back to the fact that even Disney movies such as "Cinderella" and "Sleeping Beauty" lead us to believe that girls are to be beautiful princesses and guys are to be handsome princes.

Proverbs 31 describes a dream woman. It is interesting to note that her looks are not mentioned anywhere. Today, a lot of emphasis is placed on a woman's appearance, but according to Proverbs, beauty comes from inside. What is on the inside matters more as what is on the outside.

God made us all different, in all shapes and sizes, and therefore it is unrealistic to compare yourself with others. Out of six billion people on earth, no one looks like you. You are super unique – embrace it!

Prayer

Thank you, God, that You made me unique. Help me to be myself and to accept myself.

Today's Quote

We are all born originals - why is it so many of us die copies?
—Edward Young

Understand that life can feel meaningless at times

Bible passage

Ecclesiastes 1: 1-11 *Nothing has any meaning*

1 These are the words of the Teacher. He was the son of David. He was also king in Jerusalem.

2 "Meaningless! Everything is meaningless!"
says the Teacher.
"Everything is completely meaningless!
Nothing has any meaning." *(NIrV)*

Devotion

"Everything is meaningless" is a main theme of the book that weaves through each chapter like a consistent theme.

I must admit that it is quite surprising that a Bible book on wisdom begins in such a negative fashion. How on earth could the author of this book give us hope when he is filled with so much negativity? Maybe a doctor would have diagnosed him with clinical depression.

The question we need to ask is whether we should read such a cynical book at a time that already reflects so much despair. The answer is yes; we should, because the author challenges us to think about life—our own lives. The wisdom he gives us is something he only came to realize late in life: we need to *"Have respect for God and obey his commandments. That's what everyone should do"* (12:13, NIrV).

God's commandments are about establishing healthy relationships. Only within healthy relationships do we experience a sense of belonging and community, and without that we will find it difficult to experience life as being meaningful.

Prayer

Lord, teach me to be honest with myself with You.

Today's Quote

Ever more people today have the means to live, but no meaning to live for.
— Victor Frankl

People can never serve Me and money, but they must learn to serve Me with money

Bible passage

Ecclesiastes 5: 10-12 *The Futility of Wealth*

10 *Anyone who loves money* never has enough.

Anyone who loves wealth is never satisfied with what he gets.

That doesn't have any meaning either. *(NIrV)*

Devotion

The theme of the book of Ecclesiastes (that everything is meaningless) gave the author the reputation of being a pessimist. But in this case, we have to concede that his judgment of money is realistic. He warns us in these three proverbs that the pursuit of money does not lead to happiness — in fact, the contrary is more often true.

The author gives us several reasons why he believes this to be the case. First, we will never reach the point in which we will feel that we have enough money (v. 10). Second, others (such as family and friends) will normally use up our money (v. 11). Third, it is often the very rich who will have sleepless nights about money (v. 12).

When you chase after money, you become like money — cold and clinical. Those who do not have money are normally the ones who think that money will bring them happiness. At most, money can bring comfort, but not true happiness.

Prayer

"O God, I beg two favors from you; let me have them before I die. First, help me never to tell a lie. Second, give me neither poverty nor riches! Give me just enough to satisfy my needs. For if I grow rich, I may deny you and say, 'Who is the Lord?' And if I am too poor, I may steal and thus insult God's holy name" (Prov. 30: 7-9, *NLT*).

Today's Quote

If you want to feel rich, just count the things you have that money can't buy.

– Author unknown

Grateful when people realize that that they don't need to understand everything

Bible passage

Ecclesiastes 8: 16-17

17 I realized that no one can discover everything God is doing under the sun. Not even the wisest people discover everything, no matter what they claim. *(NLT)*

Devotion

The author comes to the conclusion that one cannot understand everything in life. I agree with him wholeheartedly. I wrestle with questions like: Why are innocent people being brutally murdered? Why must there be so much suffering in the world? Why?

The author's insight thrills me. We always think that we must have the answers to all of life's questions, but this is not the case! Unfortunately, many believers sometimes create the impression that they know everything. They tend to give people who are in need easy solutions and answers. Instant answers seldom comfort those in need — in fact, they immerse others in more gloom and doom.

People often find believers who thrive on instant answers to be cold and unsympathetic. People who are in need do not always look for answers but rather for someone who will lend them an ear. Although they do not understand everything, it helps them if someone listens to them carefully and sympathetically.

Prayer

Thank You, Lord, that I do not have to understand everything in life.
Help me to listen more instead of trying to provide all the answers.

Today's Quote

Confidence, like art, never comes from having all the answers;
it comes from being open to all the questions.
— Author unknown

Aging is not for cowards!

Bible passage

Ecclesiastes 12: 1-4 *Remember God in Your Youth*

1 Remember your Creator in the days of your youth, before the days of trouble come and the years approach when you will say, "I find no pleasure in them" — *(TNIV)*

Devotion

What goes up that can never comes down? Your age! In the above passage, the author uses vivid imagery in writing about aging.

In verse 2, he describes the winter rains of Palestine: wet and depressing. This is what aging means to him. In verse 3, he describes how a person's limbs deteriorate one after the other. The "keepers" refer to the arms and hands, which previously protected the person when he fell but have now become shaky. The "strong men" refer to the legs, which walked tall and upright but now start to stagger. The "grinders" describe the teeth that chewed all the food but now, because there are few of them left, are no longer able to do that properly. The "windows" are the eyes that can no longer see as well and as far as before, making the world seem as if it has become a dark place.

Verse 4 tells us about the ears: they can no longer hear distinctly what goes on in the streets. The "sound of grinding" is the voice, which has become old and faint. Aging is not easy. For this reason, the author suggests in verse 1 that the best time to establish our relationship with God is in our youth, but it's never too late!

Prayer

Thank You, Lord, for all the young people who know You. Thank You for all the senior citizens who have known You since their childhood.

Today's Quote

When I was young I felt I had to carry the gospel; now that I am old
I know that the gospel carries me.
— Martin Niemoeller

An important tip for happiness in love to grow

Bible passage
Song of Solomon 2: 3-7 *Love Makes Everything Beautiful*
7 Promise me, O women of Jerusalem,
by the gazelles and wild deer,
not to awaken love until the time is right. *(NLT)*

Devotion
Most songs are about love—specifically, about love that has suffered loss. We all seek after love but often stumble in our search. The pain of love that has failed can be a bitter pill to swallow. So, how can our happiness in love blossom to maturity? There are many answers to this question. This section in Song of Solomon contains a handy tip.

In this passage, the poet tells us about a passionate encounter between two lovers. The woman describes how her lover stands out above all the other men (v. 3). She feels safe with him ("I sit in his delightful shade") and enjoys his caresses ("and taste his delicious fruit").

The woman interrupts her description of the encounter by asking the women of Jerusalem for a favor. Her earnest request contains an important tip for relationships: "not to awaken love until the time is right." These words mean that happiness that flows from love should develop spontaneously. It should not be forced, nor should it ripen prematurely. Love ripens prematurely when the *passion* of the embrace/caress is stronger than the *union* and commitment to each other. Our emotions and union have to develop in unison. This will let the happiness of love grow!

Prayer
Lord, help me to create space for love's happiness to grow.

Today's Quote
The sound of a kiss is not so loud as a cannon, but its echo lasts a great deal longer!
—Author unknown

happiness

If Hollywood could portray love this way

Bible passage

Song of Solomon 7
6 Oh, how beautiful you are!
How pleasing, my love, how full of delights!
7 You are slender like a palm tree,
and your breasts are like its clusters of fruit. *(NLT)*

Devotion

In this section, the lover makes it very clear that he wants to have sex with his partner. He yearns for her body and wants to caress her breasts. When she kisses him, it resembles the smell of apples and the taste of good wine—too wonderful! This union of love is exciting and special because it is exclusive. He is the only one who has the privilege to enjoy his lover's body. She does not hold back anything, since she experiences love and feels excited because he desires her and nobody else (v. 10).

Three words sum up their feelings on sex: *love, trust* and *longevity*. If either of these three is absent, sexuality cannot really flourish. How many people have not regretted the fact that they had sex when they were too young? So many people have been disillusioned because they thought that sex would guarantee their happiness.

Sex is intimate and should be protected, and love, trust and longevity create the ideal environment in which this can occur. Although this passage does not mention marriage, common sense tells us that marriage creates the best situation in which love, trust and longevity can be guaranteed.

Prayer
Lord, help me to create a safe environment for love to flourish.

Today's Quote
Sex education may be a good idea in the schools, but I don't believe the kids should be given homework.
– Bill Cosby

Wish more people realize how important it is to protect intimacy

Bible passage

Song of Solomon 8: 5-7
6 Place me like a seal over your heart,
like a seal on your arm. *(NLT)*

Devotion

We all yearn for intimacy. Knowing that we are loved and feeling that we are appreciated and cherished gives meaning to our lives. Yet in reality, many people experience rejection and loneliness. This is so unnecessary! Why did the couple in the Song of Solomon experience maturity and intimacy?

The secret to their great relationship lies in her request to her bridegroom: "*Place me like a seal* over your heart, *like a seal* on your arm." (v. 6).

In the ancient world, a man's signet ring was like a signature. It belonged to him exclusively and was, therefore, his most precious possession. The woman's request implies that she wants to feel safe with him, which requires his trust. Why would she ask this if things were going so well in their relationship? Because intimacy between two people has the potential that someone will get hurt. True intimacy will make you vulnerable because the other person will know everything about you. This vulnerability should be protected. This is why you should not rush into a relationship. You have to make sure that the degree of intimacy coincides with the degree of commitment to the relationship. Never allow someone to take you to a level of intimacy for which he or she is not prepared.

Prayer

Lord, help me to protect intimacy through commitment.

Today's Quote

Stay committed to your decisions, but stay flexible in your approach.
—Tom Robbins

The Divided Kingdom - Tweets
(925 – ± 700 BC)
(2 Kings, Jonah, Amos, Hosea, Isaiah 1-39, Micah)

▶ The kingdom divides in two.
Why? Solomon enforced heavy taxes to generate money and treated the southern tribes better than the northern tribes. The northern tribes broke away in 925 BC to form an independent kingdom. The Northern Kingdom retained the name "Israel," while the Southern Kingdom became known as "Judah."

▶ The Northern Kingdom
Northern Kingdom (Israel) consisted of 10 tribes and had 19 kings before they were taken into exile by Assyria.

▶ Southern Kingdom
The Southern Kingdom (Judah) consisted of 2 tribes and had 20 kings before they were taken into exile by Babylon.

▶ Prophets
Prophets call the kings and people to remember God's covenant and to be obedient to God or face judgment.

So thankful that my prophet Elisa heard the cry of the desperate woman

Bible passage

2 Kings 4: 1-7 *Elisha and the widow's oil*

7 She came and told the man of God, and he said, 'Go, sell the oil and pay your debts, and you and your children can live on the rest.' *(NRSV)*

Devotion

No one wants to experience emptiness, a situation of brokenness. The reality is that emptiness can be a wonderful gift. That's the lesson a destitute woman learned from the prophet Elisha.

One day Elisha meets a woman with nothing – no husband, no income, no food, and no prospects. She only had oil. The prophet tells her to collect empty jars and to pour her oil into the empty jars. She begins to pour her oil into the empty jars until all the jars are full. When she fills the last jar only then the oil of the first jar run out. The woman gets as much oil as she has empty jars.

There is something about "nothing" that moves God's hand. It is at the empty places that we learn to lean on nothing except God's provision. John Maxwell writes in "The Maxwell leadership Bible" that this story teaches us that …

1. Emptiness is a gift from the Lord
2. Emptiness tells us that we have a need.
3. It is possible that we may not be empty enough.
4. We must admit our emptiness.
5. Only God can fill us.

Prayer

God, I thank You that You fill my emptiness with Your presence.

Today's Quote

Our hearts are restless until they rest in You.
—St. Augustine

Josiah pleases My heart by leading with example

Bible passage

2 Kings 23: 1-30 *Josiah's Religious Reforms*

25 Before him there was no king like him, who turned to the Lord with all his heart, with all his soul, and with all his might, according to all the law of Moses; nor did any like him arise after him. *(NRSV)*

Devotion

The most valuable gift I can give to others is a good example. Josiah, the king of Judah (641–609 BC) instituted major reforms because he was leading by example. The public renewals implemented by Josiah were a result of the personal renewal he experienced in his own life. Public change begins with a leader's heart. When good kings lead Israel and Judah, the people were good. When bad kings led, the people went sour. Why? People do what people see. Words alone will not bring about change.   King Josiah proclaimed the need for public reform, but his words carried weight because he had experienced the change himself first. His example spoke louder than his words. The words he spoke, as a leader, were backed up by his life.

Being a good example is a responsibility all of us share – not just kings, presidents and parents. The fact is, we all are an influence on people around us, whether we're trying to be or not. Almost everything we say or do affects our friends and family, either for bad or for good. They will reject or accept our values, depending on how clearly and consistently we demonstrate our commitment. It has been said, "A pint of example is worth a gallon of advice."

Prayer

God, I realize anew the importance of setting a good example. Help me to support my words with my life.

Today's Quote

See the next page.

WHEN YOU THOUGHT I WASN'T LOOKING...
By Mary Rita Schilke Korzan

When you thought I wasn't looking you hung my first painting on the refrigerator, and I wanted to paint another.

When you thought I wasn't looking you fed a stray cat, and I thought it was good to be kind to animals.

When you thought I wasn't looking you baked a birthday cake just for me, and I knew that little things were special things.

When you thought I wasn't looking you said a prayer, and I believed there was a God that I could always talk to.

When you thought I wasn't looking you kissed me good-night, and I felt loved.

When you thought I wasn't looking I saw tears come from your eyes, and I learned that sometimes things hurt-but that it's all right to cry.

When you thought I wasn't looking you smiled, and it made me want to look that pretty, too.

When you thought I wasn't looking you cared, and I wanted to be everything I could be.

When you thought I wasn't looking-I looked . . . and wanted to say thanks for all those things you did when you thought I wasn't looking.

Aching because Jonah runs from Me

Bible passage

Jonah 1 *Jonah runs from the LORD*
14 Then they cried out to the LORD, "Please, LORD, do not let us die for taking this man's life. Do not hold us accountable for killing an innocent man, for you, LORD, have done as you pleased." *(TNIV)*

Devotion

Centuries ago, seafarers were afraid to undertake long sea voyages because they believed that the earth was flat. Our problem is that we view God's mercy in the same way as the seafarers viewed the earth. This restricted them, as they were afraid they would fall off the edge of the world. Heathen sailors in the book Jonah discovered that God's mercy is not flat but round. What does this mean?

When God told Jonah to warn the people of Nineveh to repent, he turned the opposite direction and fled to Tarshish. However, during the sea voyage to Tarshish, a heavy storm erupted. Jonah told the sailors that if they threw him overboard, the sea would calm down. These heathen sailors at first tried to row harder, but when this did not help, they prayed to Jonah's God instead.

It is ironic that heathens recognized God's absolute power by praying to Him while Jonah denied it by fleeing. The actions of these heathens affirmed that God's mercy is not flat but round. Something that is round does not have a beginning or an end. It cannot, therefore, be restricted. God's mercy is exactly like this! He saved the lives of the heathen seafarers and also that of the disobedient Jonah. His mercy also encircles us.

Prayer

Thank you, Lord, that Your mercy encircles me on all sides.

Today's Quote

I do not at all understand the mystery of grace - only that it meets us where we are but does not leave us where it found us.

—Anne Lamott

Asking Jonah, "Is it right for you to be angry?"

Bible passage

Jonah 4 *Jonah's anger at the Lord's compassion*

10 But the LORD said, "You have been concerned about this vine, though you did not tend it or make it grow. It sprang up overnight and died overnight. [11] But Nineveh has more than a hundred and twenty thousand people who cannot tell their right hand from their left, and many cattle as well. Should I not be concerned about that great city?" *(NIV)*

Devotion

Our motives determine how we react. Jonah experienced great delight when God planned to destroy the wicked people of Nineveh, but he grew angry when they repented and God showed them compassion. His selfish motives led him astray.

Jonah's problem was so ironic: He was glad because of his own salvation, but he became angry when God saved Nineveh.

Jonah wanted to die while all the heathens in the book — the sailors and the Ninevites — wanted to live. Jonah was concerned about a petty vine, yet he grew angry when God took pity on a whole city. He did not understand that God's mercy is for everybody. It cannot be kept for ourselves.

It should be our desire to be more like God than Jonah – to have God's great concern rather than Jonah's pettiness, to have God's great mercy rather than Jonah's great anger.

Prayer

Lord, save me from prejudice and selfishness. Let me not keep Your mercy all to myself!

Today's Quote

Beauty without grace is the hook without the bait.
— Ralph Waldo Emerson

Looking up to the skies and seeing the beauty of My art

Bible passage

Amos 5 *A Call to Repentance*
8 The one who made the Pleiades and Orion,
and turns deep darkness into the morning,
and darkens the day into night,
who calls for the waters of the sea,
and pours them out on the surface of the earth,
the Lord is his name, *(NRSV)*

Devotion

Living in Canada has taught me to take weather warnings seriously. To ignore them is irresponsible and can cost you your life. God wanted the Israelites to take His warnings seriously. God, therefore, pointed them to His messengers in space, the Pleiades and Orion, to show them His unlimited power.

The Pleiades, which appears in May, heralds in the beginning of summer, while the constellation of Orion, which appears in November, indicates the beginning of winter in the Northern Hemisphere. The fact that God made the Pleiades and Orion serves as proof that He controls the seasons. Furthermore, the Lord also controls the succession of day and night. He is, therefore, in control of life in all its totality. And that is not all: He also provides the rain. His omnipotence is not only evident in space and in nature but also in history (v. 9). When the vastness of creation tells us about God's greatness, it is very foolish not to take notice of God.

Prayer

Lord, I simply have to take You seriously. I praise You!

Today's Quote

The artist must be in his work as God is in creation, invisible and all-powerful; one must sense him everywhere but never see him.
— Gustave Flaubert

Wish there could have been more justice in the world

Bible passage

Amos 5 *A Call to Repentance*
12 For I know how many are your offenses
and how great your sins.
You oppress the righteous and take bribes
and you deprive the poor of justice in the courts. *(NIV)*

Devotion

Two words feature very prominently in the book of Amos. If these words find expression in people's lives, society will be a livable and safe place.

The two words that make a society livable and safe are "justice" and "righteousness." The laws of a country ensure peace within a community and the justice system is the practical application thereof.

Law and order make a society a habitable, safe and happy place in which to live. Laws and the justice system are especially meant to protect the weak, the poor and those who need help. Unfortunately, the leaders of Israel trampled on these very important institutions. Consequently, Israelite society was marked by exploitation and corruption. No corrupt society welcomes the truth, because the truth exposes injustice. God is more concerned about justice and compassion than about religious ceremony.

Christians should uphold the truth at all times, because this will ensure that justice prevails. Martin Luther King Jr. said it very well; *Injustice anywhere is a threat to justice everywhere.* We, therefore, should not be afraid to let our voice be heard.

Prayer

Lord, grant me the courage to speak up against any form of injustice.

Today's Quote

Peace is not the absence of war but the presence of justice.
—Harrison Ford

Gonna ask My prophet to do something he would never expected – to marry a prostitute

Bible passage

Hosea 1 *Hosea's family*

2 When the Lord first began speaking to Israel through Hosea, he said to him, "Go and marry a prostitute, so that some of her children will be conceived in prostitution. This will illustrate how Israel has acted like a prostitute by turning against the Lord and worshiping other gods." *(NLT)*

Devotion

People sometimes will do strange things to get a message across, like posing naked in public or going on a hunger strike. God also did a very strange thing. In order to send a clear message to the people of Israel, Hosea was to marry Gomer, a prostitute. Wow!

Hosea prophesied in Israel during a season of material wealth but spiritual poverty. God wanted his marriage to serve as visual demonstration of their unfaithfulness to Him.

God wanted them to see that in the same way Gomer had betrayed Hosea, Israel had betrayed God. We can only imagine the pain of Hosea living with the lies and deception of his wife, having to explain to his children that their mother would not come home that night.

Certainly, when Hosea spoke to the Israelites about their spiritual state, he was able to do it with passion and empathy. He knew firsthand the pain God experienced about the spiritual adultery of His chosen people. God will go to the extreme to win us back. Nothing else illustrates that better than the cross.

Prayer

Thank you, God, that You never give up on me. I love You!

Today's Quote

God loves us the way we are, but too much to leave us that way.
— Leighton Ford

Insulted by my own people. How could they?

Bible passage

Hosea 2 *Israel Punished and Restored*
13 I will punish her for the festival days of the Baals,
when she offered incense to them
and decked herself with her ring and jewellery,
and went after her lovers,
and forgot me, says the Lord. *(NRSV)*

Devotion

From birth we have been learning the rules of self-reliance as we strain and struggle to achieve self-sufficiency. These deep-seated values don't accommodate dependency on God. In fact, it pushes God aside.

This is exactly what Israel did. The Lord was hurt because His people had pushed Him aside and were following other gods. How did God react to this enormous insult?

The Lord decided to take away the hot fudge sundae and cheesecakes of their life – the nice dessert stuff – and replaced it with the hot dry place – the desert. He did not do that to punish them but to teach them that, just as the desert needs rain, we need God.

It was in the desert God was humbling them by causing them to hunger and then feeding them with manna. God was teaching them to trust in Him.

When you find yourself in the desert…you have a choice: seek a way out as fast as possible or seek the Person who wants to be your first love. Remember: The desert won't last forever; but the desert must come first…then the Promised Land.

Prayer

Lord, I want to profess my dependence on You once more.

Today's Quote

What makes the desert beautiful is that somewhere it hides a well.
— Antoine de Saint-Exupery

Amazed that they think they can fool me with their religious acts

Bible passage

Isaiah 1 *A Message for Rebellious Nation*
11 *I have had enough of burnt-offerings of rams*
and the fat of fed beasts;
I do not delight in the blood of bulls,
or of lambs, or of goats. *(NRSV)*

Devotion

Gandhi once said: "I like your Christ, I do not like your Christians. Your Christians are so unlike your Christ." Do you agree? Christians who "profess what they don't possess" — who are phony, empty, and hollow to the core have done a lot of damage to Christianity.

God is more angered by hypocrisy than we can ever be. Isaiah, therefore, flatly told the religious leaders that the Lord despised their religion because it is not accompanied by an honest life. The worst part is that they thought they could fool the Lord.

A rather pompous-looking deacon was endeavouring to impress upon a class of boys the importance of living the Christian life. "Why do people call me a Christian?" the man asked. After a moment's pause, one youngster said, "Maybe it's because they don't know you."

Robert Redford was walking one day through a hotel lobby. A woman saw him and followed him to the elevator. "Are you the real Robert Redford?" she asked him with great excitement. As the doors of the elevator closed, he replied, "Only when I am alone!" (Maybe he was just joking)

Prayer
Lord, I want to live my life in such a way that it honors You!

Today's Quote
Better to be known as a sinner than a hypocrite.
—Proverb

What will happen if people no longer dream?

Bible passage

Isaiah 35 *Hope for Restoration*
1 *The wilderness and the dry land* shall be glad,
the desert shall rejoice and blossom;
like the crocus [2] it shall blossom abundantly,
and rejoice with joy and singing. *(NRSV)*

Devotion

"I Have a Dream" is the famous name given to the ten minute public speech by Martin Luther King, Jr., in which he called for racial equality and an end to discrimination. It was that dream for a better life that changed the way people think. This is exactly why we need dreams – to have hope and to aim to change our present situation for the better.

Israel also had dreams of living peacefully in the Promised Land. But then, everything changed because of their disobedience. Their dreams turned into a nightmare when Isaiah passed judgment on Israel instead of their enemies. But then, Isaiah 35 came as sunshine after the rain. Isaiah pronounces that Israel would once again become a blooming garden (vv. 1-2). God wanted them to dream again!

My kids love Hannah Montana and I really liked Hannah Montana: The Movie. Her song, "The Climb" inspires me every time when I hear that voice inside me saying that I will never reach my dream.

And I, I got to be strong
Just keep pushing on'
Cause there's always gonna be another mountain
(Words from The Climb: Written by Jessi Alexander and Jon Mabe)

Prayer

Lord, help me to hold on to my dreams.

Today's Quote

Dreams have only one owner at a time. That's why dreamers are lonely.
— Erma Bombeck

Told Micah to proclaim good news in the midst of disappointment

Bible passage
Micah 5 *A Promised ruler from Bethlehem*
2 "But you, Bethlehem Ephrathah,
though you are small among the clans of Judah,
out of you will come for me
one who will be ruler over Israel,
whose origins are from of old,
from ancient times." *(TNIV)*

Devotion
People will spend lots of money on external things, like clothes, to portray a certain image. People want to be cool. God does not bother much about a cool image. God is more concerned about your character. Your image is about what other people think of you while character tells who you really are. God is interested in the real thing.

In Micah's time, the kings really messed up. Fortunately, Micah prophesied that the Israelites would get a king of good character who will not disappoint them. He will come from Bethlehem. At the time, Bethlehem was one of the smallest and most unimportant (uncool) places in Israel and Judah. If God considered reputation important, this king would have come from a prominent tribe and city.

God's approach tells us something: He can perform great and important things by using the most improbable things. God looks beyond the shadow (image) to the real thing.

Prayer
God, help me to pay more attention to building my character.

Today's Quote
Character is like a tree and reputation like a shadow. The shadow is what we think of it; the tree is the real thing.
— Abraham Lincoln

Thankful to Micah for the wonderful poetry explaining to the world who I am

Bible passage

Micah 7: 14-20 *Prayer and Praise*
18 Who is a God like you,
who pardons sin and forgives the transgression
of the remnant of his inheritance?
You do not stay angry forever
but delight to show mercy. *(TNIV)*

Devotion

What makes God so unique and unequalled? Micah uses wonderful poetry to explain why the God of the Bible is this way.

The book of Micah begins on a low point with God accusing His people of sinning but ends on a high point: a song of praise to God! What happens between these two points? God forgives the people of their sins and subsequently opens up new beginnings for them.

The fact that God can act in this way makes Him unique and unequalled. That is why verse 18 starts with a rhetorical question: "Who is a God like You?" The question is a wonderful wordplay on Micah's name, which is an abbreviation of "Micaiah," meaning, "Who is like the Lord?" Micah's name thus proclaims that no one is like the Lord.

God's forgiveness always opens up a new beginning. By forgiving each other, we also create an opportunity for a fresh start among ourselves. Like Micah, we can also ask with joy in our hearts, "Who is a God like You?"

Prayer

Thank You, Lord, that Your forgiveness heralds in a new beginning for me.

Today's Quote

To err is human, to forgive is divine.
— Alexander Pope

The last years of Israel and Judah – Tweets
(± 700 – ± 600 BC)
(Nahum, Zephaniah, Jeremiah and Lamentations)

▶ 722 BC: The End of the Northern Kingdom

The Israelites continued to sin against God and ignored the warnings of the prophets. After the Assyrians conquered them, the Israelites of the Northern Kingdom were taken into exile, never to return. After the Israelites were exiled, the Assyrians sent foreigners from different parts of the kingdom to inhabit the land (2 Kings 17:24), a practice that was meant to prevent uprisings in the conquered territories. The foreigners married the few Israelites who were not displaced, and this mixed race of Israelites and foreigners became known as the Samaritans.

▶ 586BC: The End of the Southern Kingdom

The Assyrian kingdom collapsed suddenly and unexpectedly in 622 BC when Media and Babylon (modern-day southern Iraq) conquered Nineveh, the capital of Assyria. Babylon then became the new world power. More than a century after the fall of Israel, Jehoiakim, the king of Judah, acted foolishly and rose up against Babylon. Nebuchadnezzar, the king of Babylon, struck back forcefully against Jerusalem in 598 BC. Then the unthinkable happened: Jerusalem, the capital of Judah, was invaded and destroyed by Babylon in 586 BC.

The people's persistent sins, despite all the warnings by the prophets, had caused the Lord to allow Jerusalem and the Temple to be destroyed (2 Kings 24:8–25:1).

No need worrying because I'm still in control

Bible passage

Nahum 1 *The Lord 's Anger Against Nineveh*
3 The LORD is slow to anger but great in power;
the LORD will not leave the guilty unpunished.
His way is in the whirlwind and the storm,
and clouds are the dust of his feet. *(TNIV)*

Devotion

"God is in control" so easily sounds like a cliché, especially when you see all the suffering in this world. For many people (sometimes I doubt as well) it doesn't feel as if God is always in control. Maybe the people of Judah must have felt the same when they, as God's people, suffered at the hands of the cruel Assyrians, the superpower at the time.

The name Nahum means "comfort," which is precisely what this book is about, and exactly what we need when we feel discourage.
Nahum makes us intensely aware of God's inconceivable majesty-especially where nature is concerned (vv. 3-5). God is in control in ways we that won't always understand.

Judah needed to know that God Almighty did not condone everything in the name of love—especially not the abuse of power that the mighty Assyrians were guilty of committing.

Jesus said: *"I am the Alpha and the Omega, the First and the Last, the Beginning and the End"* (Rev 22: 13 *NIV*). It is very comforting to know that we are not heading towards a hopeless end, but rather, towards an endless hope. When I let go, God is in control.

Prayer

God, I don't need to fear because You are my refuge and strength.

Today's Quote

Some see a hopeless end, while others see an endless hope.
— Author Unknown

Can't stand the cruelty of Nineveh anymore. Something needs to be done!

Bible passage

Nahum 3 *The Lord's Judgment against Nineveh*
19 Nothing can heal you;
your wound is fatal.
All who hear the news about you;
clap their hands at your fall,
for who has not felt
your endless cruelty? *(TNIV)*

Devotion

Jonah preached in Nineveh 150 years before Nahum (c. 633-612 BC) came on the scene. Jonah's message brought about a renewal in the nation. Now, many years later, Nahum announces the destruction of the very same Nineveh. What went wrong? Nineveh became mighty and unfortunately failed the test of character. What was this test of character? Abraham Lincoln put it very well when he said, *"Nearly all men can stand adversity, but if you want to test a man's character, give him power."*

In a sense, we are all in a position of power and authority. Within families everyone – even little people – exercise power. Kids have the power to yell for attention, and they probably get it! In marriages one may use the tongue (or withholding sex) to exercise power; the other partner may respond with silent treatment. Our character will be determined by the way we handle power. Since power can easily lead us astray, we need to be responsible with it.

Prayer

Lord, I realize anew that I need to be very careful with power.

Today's Quote

When the power of love overcomes the love of power,
the world will know peace.
—Jimi Hendrix

Ask Zephaniah to proclaim the coming judgment against Judah

Bible passage
Zephaniah 1 *Coming Judgment against Judah*
7 Be silent before the Sovereign LORD,
for the day of the LORD is near.
The LORD has prepared a sacrifice;
he has consecrated those he has invited. *(TNIV)*

Devotion
It is possible to believe theoretically but in practice to be an atheist. You can worship God on a Sunday but during the week live in such a way as if God is inactive and uninvolved and therefore cannot make any difference. This exactly how the people of Judah lived.

Zephaniah was a brilliantly creative writer who lived in Judah round about 630 BC, during the last years of the mighty Assyrian kingdom. During this time, God's people practiced idolatrous customs in secret. The perception of this hypocrisy stirred the young prophet to action. As a word artist, he paints a very strange picture.

Zephaniah paints a picture of a strange religious service with a disturbing sermon. The members of the congregation (Judah) had been invited to a sacrificial feast, only to discover that they were the sacrifice. Those who thought they were saved rudely discovered that they were actually lost. The problem was that they attended religious services on the holy day but exploited people during the week. Ken Owen said: "Always remember that your words regarding Christ will never compensate for what your life does NOT say about Him."

Prayer
Lord, let me live my words.

Today's Quote
I once wanted to become an atheist, but I gave up – they have no holidays.
—Henry Youngman

There will come a time that Jerusalem will call on My name and be saved

Bible passage
Zephaniah 3: 9-20 *Jerusalem's restoration*
9 "Then I will purify the lips of the peoples,
that all of them may call on the name of the LORD
and serve him shoulder to shoulder. *(TNIV)*

Devotion
Good prospects for the future put a smile on our faces. Without a future and without hope, no one can live a meaningful life. Judah faces judgment but Zephaniah paints a picture where God's love will triumph judgment. He was bringing something of the future into the present. Our own lives should also bring something of the future into the present in order to give others hope. But how do we do this?

Maybe my friend's story could help us. He once told me that he attended a special evening for parents at a prestigious high school where his daughter attended. The reason was to discuss the concerns they had about their kids – the increase of drug – and alcohol abuse!

At that evening parents had the opportunity to share their views. The focus was on the kids and how bad things were. My friend stood up and in his kind way wanted to change the focus by asking: "Have you ever thought what our kids think when they hear how we complain about how bad things are in politics and in the country? Have you ever wondered how kids feel when they hear how we talk? No wonder our kids turn to drugs." He wanted to make the point that what we say and do opens or closes the future.

Prayer
Lord, let my way of life help that a bit of the future shines through!

Today's Quote
The future belongs to those who give the next generation reason for hope.
— Pierre Teilhard de Chardin

Asking Jeremiah to speak at the temple, but don't think they will like his message

Bible passage

Jeremiah 7: 1-11 *Jeremiah Speaks at the Temple*

8 Here you are, trusting in deceptive words to no avail. ⁹Will you steal, murder, commit adultery, swear falsely, make offerings to Baal, and go after other gods that you have not known, ¹⁰and then come and stand before me in this house, which is called by my name, and say, 'We are safe!' —only to go on doing all these abominations? *(NRSV)*

Devotion

Church services can uplift and empower us but the reality is that it can be dangerous. Jeremiah's sermon made it very clearly that churchgoers could easily develop a false sense of security.

The people of Judah were under the impression that as long as the Temple stood, they would be safe. This religious ease caused them to lose their admiration for God, because they took His love and care for granted. They exploited those who were vulnerable: the foreigners, the orphans and the widowers. They were also guilty of theft, murder, adultery and deceit (v. 9).

The worst part is that this lifestyle did not bother them. After all, they went to the Temple. Because of this, Jeremiah had to speak to them (and to us) clearly. His message to them was that service to their neighbor was just as important as attending a religious service. The two cannot be separated. The danger is that we can easily pacify our conscience by thinking; At *least I attended the church service.* Being a Christian entails a way of life that lasts all week.

Prayer

Lord, I want to commit myself anew to serving You and people.

Today's Quote

Your religion is what you do when the sermon is over.
—H. Jackson Brown, Jr.

Telling Jeremiah that his prayer does not move me. Trust that he will understand

Bible passage

Jeremiah 15 *God will not relent*

1 Then the Lord said to me: Though Moses and Samuel stood before me, yet my heart would not turn towards this people. Send them out of my sight, and let them go! *(NRSV)*

Devotion

We believe that prayer is powerful and can change things. In this section, Jeremiah pleaded with the Lord for deliverance on behalf of the people. The people were in the midst of a severe drought. However, his prayer was flawed. Although his lamentation contained all the elements of a prayer, the Lord was not moved by it. Why?

Its weakness was not in the words he used but in the people's deeds. Their words were not consistent with their deeds.

It is of no use to rend your clothes and not your heart (Joel 2:13). If repentance lacks sincerity, nothing will help—not even the pleas of two of the greatest prophets, Moses and Samuel. The only option that remained was judgment (Jer. 15:2). Prayer should, therefore, never be taken lightly. We have to be sincere in our prayers and make sure that our prayers are always consistent with our deeds. Sincere prayers—in which deeds and words link up—move God's heart!

Prayer

Lord, I confess that I am often not serious enough about prayer.

Today's Quote

Prayer may not change things for you, but it for sure changes you for things.
—Samuel M. Shoemaker

Aching heart and eyes filled with tears

Bible passage

Jeremiah 48: 26-47 *The Sheer Nothingness of Moab*

29-33 "We've all heard of Moab's pride,

that legendary pride,

The strutting, bullying, puffed-up pride,

the insufferable arrogance.

But I will weep for Moab,

yes, I will mourn for the people of Moab.

I will even mourn for the people of Kir-heres. *(MSG)*

Devotion

It is not strange to see people cry, but it is strange to think that God can cry. After all, God is the almighty. However, this section confirms that God can indeed cry. But what would cause God to cry?

Arrogance does something to God — it makes Him cry. Why would God cry about arrogance? Arrogance is human beings' way of saying to God that they can do without Him and their neighbors. Arrogance is an indication that we do not need anybody or anything, and is probably one of the greatest stumbling blocks that prevent us from responding to God's call. This is the reason why God hates arrogance.

What causes this arrogance? It is a quest for freedom, but a freedom that is away from God, without any need to have God in our lives. To be arrogant is to be foolish, because it leads to self-destruction. It would be wise to take the following wisdom to heart: "First pride, then the crash — the bigger the ego, the harder the fall" (Prov. 16:18, *MSG*).

Prayer

Lord, I realize again how dangerous arrogance is and that it causes You so much pain.

Today's Quote

Arrogance and snobbism live in adjoining rooms and use a common currency.

—Morley Safer

arrogance

Jerusalem's cry is almost unbearable

Bible passage

Lamentations 1 *Sorrow in Jerusalem*
1 How lonely sits the city
that once was full of people!
How like a widow she has become,
she that was great among the nations!
She that was a princess among the provinces
has become a vassal. *(NRSV)*

Devotion

Sorrow is part of life. We cannot wish it away but rather focus on how to escape from the depths of one's own sorrow. This passage can be helpful.

The book of Lamentations mourns the destruction of Jerusalem by the Babylonians in 586 BC. In this passage, Jerusalem is portrayed as a woman who once enjoyed prestige but now cries bitterly over her misery. She has been stripped of her dignity. Her pain is aggravated because there is no one to comfort her. The fall of Jerusalem led to the collapse of the people's religious life. Had the Lord forgotten them? Why did she have to suffer so much? Yet the people would discover soon enough that their suffering did not imply God's rejection.

It was the custom, in the Old East, to sing lamentations when someone died or during serious illness or a major tragedy. This song is an invitation to you to bemoan your own pain to the Lord. We don't need to hide our true feelings. Unexpressed emotions could easily lead to depression. Honesty toward God opens the way to escape the depths of sorrow.

Prayer
Thank You, Lord, that I can bring my sorrow to You.

Today's Quote
Honesty prospers in every condition of life.
—Johann Friedrich Von Schiller

You can count on My steadfast love

Bible passage

Lamentations 3 *Hope in the Lord's Faithfulness*
21 But this I call to mind,
and therefore I have hope:
²² The steadfast love of the Lord never ceases,
his mercies never come to an end;
²³they are new every morning;
great is your faithfulness.
²⁴ 'The Lord is my portion,' says my soul,
'therefore I will hope in him.' *(NRSV)*

Devotion

We do not look for hope in the light, when things are going well. That is not the place where we became hopeless. Instead, we look for hope where we lost it—where it is dark. Yet in his darkest hour, this poet experienced a change of mind.

The word "but" in verse 21 indicates that the poet's state of mind has changed. This happened when he shifted his focus away from himself to God. He realizes that he is still alive and that he did not perish because of God's love. He also realizes that his suffering does not imply rejection.

Hope means that we have a tomorrow (morning), and those who have a tomorrow also have a today. If we know that we will still have a job tomorrow, we can live with hope today. If you find yourself at a dark place, go and talk to someone. You may have lost much but you never need to lose hope. Hope is the fuel that propels us into the future.

Prayer

Lord, thank You that I am assured that You are part of my life, even in my darkest hour.

Today's Quote

Hope is the last thing ever lost.
—Italian proverb

The Exile and Return – Tweets
(± 597 – ± 420 BC)
(Habakkuk, Obadiah, Isaiah 40-66, Ezekiel, Daniel, Haggai, Zechariah, Joel, Esther, Ezra, Nehemiah, Malachi)

▶ The Exile (597–538 BC)

The exile changed the people's way of worshipping. Because they were now far away from Jerusalem, the Temple and sacrifices could no longer be the focal point of their worship. Instead, prayer, confession and teaching became the focus of their worship. The gatherings in their homes preceded the assemblies in the synagogues. The Temple priests who were also taken into exile acted as interpreters of the Law.

▶ The Return (538 – 420 BC)

In 549 B.C., Cyrus the Great founded the Persian Empire, and he eventually conquered Babylon. Persia was now the new world power.

The two centuries the Persians reigned were of great importance to God's people, as the Persians encouraged their repatriation and also subsidized it.

* The first group of exiles returned with Sheshbazzar (538 B.C.), an exiled Jewish prince and later governor of a reestablished Jewish state centered in Jerusalem.

* A little later Zerubabel, the grandson of king Jehoiachin, escorted another group back to the homeland.

* The next main group returned in 458 B.C. with Ezra, the scribe.

* Then in 444 B.C., Nehemiah returned with another group.

It was during this time that the exiles who returned home were called "Jews" for the first time. This word derives from the Hebrew word Yehudi, which is related to Judah, the tribe in which Jesus was born.

Habakkuk's honesty really moved Me

Bible passage

Habakkuk 1: 1-4 *Habakkuk's Complaint*
2 How long, LORD, must I call for help, *but you do not listen?*
Or cry out to you, 'Violence!' *but you do not save? (TNIV)*

Devotion

Why do good people have to suffer so much? Why do bad things happen to us? If God is love, why is there so much suffering? All of us wrestle with these questions at one point or another.

Habakkuk wrestled with the same questions. Habakkuk experienced a religious crisis when the Babylonians destroyed Jerusalem (568 BC). Everything on which the people depended collapsed with the fall of Jerusalem: the kingdom of David, the Temple in Jerusalem and the belief that they were God's special people.

Habakkuk grappled with God about real-life issues. He experienced tension between reality and faith. What he saw and experienced made it difficult for him to cling to God's promises and maintain his faith. His questions reflected bewilderment, but not unbelief. That is why he put his questions to God. We are invited to join Habakkuk in his struggle, because by struggling, we discover the extent of God's mercy.

Habakkuk means "to embrace," and he earned the title by wrestling with God in the beginning of his book and by developing deep intimacy with God by the book's end.

Prayer
The Sovereign LORD is my strength;
He makes my feet like the feet of a deer,
He enables me to tread on the heights. (Hab 3: 19 *TNIV*)

Today's Quote
Judge a person by their questions, rather than their answers.
—Voltaire

Cannot believe that Edom could do that to Israel

Bible passage

Obadiah 1 *Edom's Judgment Announced*
12 *You should not gloat over your brother*
in the day of his misfortune,
nor rejoice over the people of Judah
in the day of their destruction,
nor boast so much
in the day of their trouble. *(TNIV)*

Devotion

One of the worst things that can ever happen to anyone is to be backstabbed. It is such a devastating experience when you have put your trust in someone and to find out that you have been betrayed. This is exactly what the people of Judah experienced.

Obadiah, the shortest book in the Old Testament, announced judgment on Edom because they *betrayed* their brother, Israel and took pleasure in their misfortune. The Edomites were in cahoots with Judah's enemy and contributed to the downfall of their brother. When Babylon invaded Judah and destroyed Jerusalem in 587 BC, the Edomites rejoiced in their misfortune (v. 12). Because Judah was disobedient their punishment was justified, but Edom's arrogance and betrayal went against God's sense of justice and honor. God therefore punished them (v. 15).

The challenge is to be what Obadiah's name means: "Servant of the Lord." As the Lord's servants, we need to forgive those who have backstabbed us and be trustworthy people. George Macdonald said "to be trusted is a greater compliment than being loved."

Prayer

Lord, make me humble and help me to be trusted.

Today's Quote

Betrayal is the only truth that sticks.
— Arthur Miller

Think the Israelites will be shocked to hear that the Persian king is an anointed one

Bible passage

Isaiah 45 *Cyrus, the Lord's Chosen On*
1 "This is what the LORD says to his anointed,
to Cyrus, whose right hand I take hold of
to subdue nations before him and to strip kings of their armor,
to open doors before him so that gates will not be shut: *(TNIV)*

Devotion

What do we do when God just doesn't seem to make sense? This section gave me a better understanding of God. Isaiah is about the Israelites who are in exile, but will eventually be freed and will return to Jerusalem. God put a unique plan in motion to achieve this. This unique plan must have shocked those who first heard about it. Why?

The Israelites heard that the Lord would use someone who was anointed to free them from exile. They must have been shocked to hear that it would be Cyrus, the Persian king. He did not know the Lord and was not an Israelite. This was the first and only time that a non-Israelite received the title of the anointed—the "messiah." Like us, the Israelites had to realize that the Lord couldn't be limited.

God works in unexpected ways. This confirms that He alone is God and that He determines the cause of events. The Lord enabled Cyrus to be extremely successful. Cyrus conquered Babylonia and allowed the Israelites to return to Jerusalem. Today, God still works in ways that we do not understand because *He alone is God!*

Prayer

Lord, it is liberating to know that You are in control in a unique way.

Today's Quote

A religion without mystery must be a religion without God.
—Jeremy Taylor

Jerusalem not to worry - glory on its way

Bible passage

Isaiah 60 *Future Glory for Jerusalem*
1 "Arise, shine, for your light has come,
and the glory of the LORD rises upon you. *(TNIV)*

Devotion

A well-known Jewish legend tells about two rabbis who sat and argued whether the Messiah had already come to earth. They quoted the Scriptures and the sages and peppered each other with arguments. In an attempt to settle the argument, one of them walked to the window and said to the other, "Look outside! Look at the state of the world. If the Messiah had already come, it would not look the way it does." This rabbi believed that seeing is believing.

The disillusioned exiles that returned to Jerusalem also believed like that rabbi. All they could see through their windows were ruins, suffering and misery. Isaiah wanted to teach them to look beyond the ruins of Jerusalem. They had to see that God was once again committed to them. God sees beyond what we see; God sees the destination.

It can be compared to a dog owner who uses his finger to point out the spot where his dog should fetch the ball. Where does the dog look? The dog usually keeps his eyes on the owner's finger. The owner wants the dog to start moving in the direction he is pointing, but the dog does not grasp this. All we see is God's "finger" pointing to a destination.

Many says, "Seeing is believing." Christ says, "Believing is seeing." Hebrews 11:1: "Now faith is being sure of what we hope for and certain of what we do not see" *(TNIV)*.

Prayer

Lord, I believe that we are heading towards an endless hope!

Today's Quote

Some things have to be believed to be seen.
—Ralph Hodgson

Show Ezekiel my glory while he is in Babylon among the exiles

Bible passage

Ezekiel 1 *A vision*

1 In my thirtieth year, ... while I was among the exiles by the Kebar River, the heavens were opened and I saw visions of God. *(TNIV)*

Devotion

Where is God? Have you ever asked that question? Most of us have at one time or another. Its answer has more to do with God's presence in our lives than with belief in God's existence. We want to know - where is God when something goes desperately wrong in my life?

The exiles in Babylon felt exactly the same. They thought that God resided in the Temple in Jerusalem, but they were in Babylon—about 500 miles (about 800 kilometers) away. They felt that this was their darkest hour. Yet, it was during this darkest period of the Old Testament that something surprising happened.

More than 500 miles away from Jerusalem, in the enemy's territory, God appeared to Ezekiel in a vision. This vision made Ezekiel realize that God was not restricted to the four walls of a Temple. There, in the enemy's territory, God used this vision to say to Ezekiel, "I am not far from you." While the people had their doubts about God, He was the One who went to call on them.

Where is God? A rabbi once answered this question by saying that God is where people look for Him, because He is already looking for them.

Prayer
Lord, I thank You that you are with me all the time!

Today's Quote
Maybe the atheist cannot find God for the same reason a thief cannot find a policeman.
— Author Unknown

where is God?

Ask Ezekiel to raise a funeral song over Tyre

Bible passage

Ezekiel 27 *A Funeral Song for Tyre*
1 The word of the LORD came to me: [2] "Son of man, take up a lament concerning Tyre. *(TNIV)*

Devotion

On Thursday, the April 11, 1912, the most famous passenger liner in the world at the time, the Titanic, left Queenstown harbor on its maiden voyage across the Atlantic ocean to New York. Four days later, the *New York Times* carried the heading: "Titanic Sinks Four Hours After Hitting Iceberg." More than 1,500 people died in that disaster, among them the world richest man. These events were relived in the successful 1997 movie called *Titanic*.

The Bible had its own Titanic. Unfortunately, it also sank. Not a movie, but a sad song describes the end of the Bible's Titanic. Here we have the picture of a mighty ship sailing through the waters. A luxury ship represents the prosperous trading city of Tyre. Tyre was the Bible's Titanic. Like the Titanic, it had no equal. It played a leading naval role in the region, had partners everywhere, and was significant in the world market. Unfortunately, the people of Tyre used Jerusalem's destruction to their own advantage. Moving imagery in this passage predicts their end.

God does not tolerate enrichment at the expense of others because it disturbs the SHALOM God wants to see on earth. The Hebrew word SHALOM is understood to mean peace. But it also means well-being, welfare or safety of others. Have you ever asked yourself under what circumstances the people work who make the brands we wear?

Prayer

Lord, help me never to exploit others and always to seek justice.

Today's Quote

Professionals built the Titanic, amateurs the ark.
— Frank Pepper

Taking Ezekiel on the ride of his life

Bible passage

Ezekiel 40 *The New Temple Area Restored*

2 In a vision from God he took me to the land of Israel and set me down on a very high mountain. From there I could see toward the south what appeared to be a city. *(NLT)*

Devotion

We have all encountered dark times in our lives. Dark times tend to rob us of something we cannot do without, namely, *hope*. God used Ezekiel in a wonderful way to give His exiled people new hope.

Fourteen years after the destruction of Jerusalem, God took Ezekiel there in a vision – the ride of his life! Ezekiel was ordered to look and listen well—and to tell Israel what he saw and heard. Ezekiel saw the Temple and was overwhelmed by its greatness. The Temple of the Lord outshone all previous buildings. It is described as inconceivable.

The description of the Temple reflects much more than the description of a building—it reflects how the prophet experienced the greatness, steadfastness, majesty and trustworthiness of God.

God used this vision to let Ezekiel know that even though the exiles were in an hour of great darkness, *He was still the Lord*! This expression is repeated 54 times in the book. God used this vision to tell His people that their misery would come to an end.

Ezekiel's name means "God will strengthen." May the meaning of his name be a source of hope in times of darkness?

Prayer

Lord, I join Ezekiel in confessing that You are our strength.

Today's Quote

When things are bad, we take comfort in the thought that they could always get worse. And when they are, we find hope in the thought that things are so bad they have to get better.

—Malcolm Forbes

Show solidarity with Shadrach, Meshach and Abednego in the blazing furnace

Bible passage

Daniel 3 *Shadrach, Meshach, and Abednego*

17 If the God we serve is able to deliver us, then he will deliver us from the blazing furnace and from Your Majesty's hand. [18] But even if he does not, we want you to know, Your Majesty, that we will not serve your gods or worship the image of gold you have set up." *(TNIV)*

Devotion

A young soldier who had a steady girlfriend in the town where he lived admitted to his chaplain that he would never date any other girl if he were within a radius of 50 miles from his home. His loyalty had a reach of only 50 miles! How far does your loyalty reach, especially where God is concerned?

When reading the stories of the three friends in the furnace and Daniel in the lion's den, we cannot help but wonder why God would save them but not the believers in Hitler's gas chambers and furnaces. We will never know for sure. It is interesting to note that the three friends did consider the fact that they could die. "But even if he does not, we want you to know, Your Majesty, that we will not serve your gods" (v. 18). They displayed a loyalty that is so admirable. Woodrow T. Wilson said that loyalty means nothing unless it has at its heart the absolute principal of self-sacrifice.

True loyalty to God always includes helping those in need. Jesus told his disciples, 'I tell you the truth, whatever you did not do for one of the least of these, you did not do for me.' (Matt 25: 45 *NIV*)

Prayer

God, I want to declare my loyalty to You anew.

Today's Quote

One loyal friend is worth ten thousand relatives

—Euripides

Thrilled that a heathen king praises My Name

Bible passage

Daniel 4: 34-37 *Nebuchadnezzar Praises God*
37 Now I, Nebuchadnezzar, praise and exalt and glorify the King of
heaven, because everything he does is right and all his ways are just. And
those who walk in pride he is able to humble. *(TNIV)*

Devotion

God wants us to glorify and praise Him as the almighty God. However,
there is one characteristic—a vice—that prevents us from doing this
wholeheartedly. Arrogance prevents us from glorifying and praising God,
because when we are arrogant, we only praise ourselves.

Nebuchadnezzar, king of Babylon, was very arrogant and wicked to the
poor. But when he discovered his shortcomings from the interpretation of
a dream and confessed, the mighty king erupted in praise.
Nebuchadnezzar's whole experience is told in Daniel 4 in the form of a
letter that he sent throughout his kingdom.

Some scholars maintain that the book of Daniel was concluded during
the time of the arrogant Greek king Antiochus IV Epiphanes (175-164 BC),
who made the Jews' lives very unpleasant. It must have been very
comforting for them to know that God's could do the same to Antiochus IV
Epiphanes as He did to Nebuchadnezzar.

We live in totally different times from those who first read the book, but
we should remember that none of the writers of the Bible considered
arrogance a virtue. As Proverbs 29:23 states, "*Pride* brings a person low, *but
the lowly in spirit* gain honor" *(TNIV)*.

Prayer

Lord, save me from arrogance. I always want to praise and honor You!

Today's Quote

*A proud man is always looking down on things and people; and, of course, as
long as you're looking down, you can't see something that's above you.*
—C.S. Lewis

Daniel saw a vision that gave the Jews hope

Bible passage
Daniel 12 *Daniel's Vision of a Ram and a Goat*
13 "As for you, go your way till the end. You will rest, and then at the end of the days you will rise to receive your allotted inheritance." *(TNIV)*

Devotion
The uncertainty of the future scares many people. That is why change is often traumatic because you need to leave your comfort zone.

Scholars believe that the first readers of Daniel lived under severe persecution and were worried about their future. The first readers were the Jews, suffering at the hand of Antiochus IV Epiphanes, the cruel Greek leader, who forced the Greek culture on the Jews.

God understands uncertainty and gave the people hope through visions. Visions give you a glimpse of the future. The power of visions is that it helps you to view the present in the light of the future. Visions helped these sorrowful Jews to look beyond their situation and to see God as the one who was in control.

Daniel did not understand what the outcome of this vision would be (v. 8). He tried to find out, but the angel reminded him that the end of time is a secret (v. 9). The angel's directive to Daniel in the closing verse (v.13) inspired many of the Jews, during the reign of Antiochus, to strive toward the future. The Bible makes it very clear that the future belongs to God.

Daniel means "God is my judge" and it is just another way to say that God is in control. We can be so obsessed with the future that we can miss out on the present blessings. Today is all that you have! Enjoy!

Prayer
Thank You, Lord that You are already in the future.

Today's Quote
The best thing about the future is that it comes only one day at a time.
— Abraham Lincoln

Asking Haggai to talk earnestly to the exiles

Bible passage

Haggai 1 *A Call to Build the House of the LORD*
3 Then the word of the LORD came through the prophet Haggai: 4 'Is it a time for you yourselves to be living in your paneled houses, while this house remains a ruin?' *(TNIV)*

Devotion

Haggai was the first prophet to appear on the scene after the Lord's people began to return to Judah from exile (August 29, 520 BC – December 18, 520 BC). During this time, the people were making all kinds of excuses for not completing the Temple. People can be very inventive when conjuring up excuses. Haggai's message exposes the reason behind many of them.

As the story goes, the captain of the Titanic at some stage told his crew, "Now it is every man for himself!" This is often people's reaction when things get tough. Self-interest becomes the highest priority. This is exactly what Haggai exposed as the reason behind all the people's excuses. They took the trouble to look after their own houses but had neglected the house of the Lord (v. 4). They had put their own interests before God's interests.

We can be very inventive when we conjure up excuses, but perhaps we should learn to be honest with others and ourselves. When I need to turn something down I have learnt to say something like, "I need to be realistic. I will be unable to attend." This helps me not to find excuses.

Jules Renard said, "The only man who is really free is the one who can turn down an invitation to dinner without giving an excuse."

Prayer

Lord, I confess that self-interest often lies behind my excuses.

Today's Quote

An excuse is worse than a lie, for an excuse is a lie, guarded.
— Alexander Pope

Talk to Zechariah through night visions

Bible passage

Zechariah 4 *The Fifth vision*

10 "Who dares despise the day of small things, since the seven eyes of the LORD that range throughout the earth will rejoice when they see the chosen capstone in the hand of Zerubbabel?" *(TNIV)*

Devotion

Zechariah became a prophet in 520 BC, shortly after Haggai. The first part of the book (1–8) tells us about eight night visions Zechariah had. In the fifth night vision God made it clear that bigger is not always better.

Many Jews were disappointed when they realized that the second temple would not be as spectacular as Solomon's Temple. To them, bigger and more beautiful meant better. They had to learn that God is not concerned about what is bigger and more beautiful but, rather, about what is right. That is why God asks, *"Who dares despise the day of small things?"* (v.10). God expects us to be faithful in small things, which enables Him to perform great things in our lives. God's way of doing things often starts off small, but the results end up big. The rebuilding of the Temple was a small effort by a small group of people, but its consequences were important.

Although the second Temple was less spectacular than that of Solomon, it was more important that the people had a central place of worship after all their years in exile.

It is so easy to disregard the little things in life. In reality it is *every* small thing that makes the biggest difference in our lives.

Prayer

Lord, help me to do small things as if they were great.

Today's Quote

Be faithful in small things because it is in them that your strength lies.
—Mother Teresa of Calcutta

Request Zechariah to ask the people if they really fasted for Me

Bible passage

Zechariah 7 *Question about fasting*
5 "Ask all the people of the land and the priests, 'When you fasted and mourned in the fifth and seventh months for the past seventy years, was it really for me that you fasted? *(TNIV)*

Devotion

What do you think of when you hear the word "tradition"? This question is very relevant, especially in the Church, where tradition plays a very important role. Some want to embrace tradition where others despise it. How do we need to approach tradition? This passage will help us to understand how to approach tradition.

Two years before the Temple was completed, a delegation from the town of Bet-El, located about 11 miles (18 kilometers) north of Jerusalem, went to Jerusalem with a specific request. They wanted to find out whether it was still significant to commemorate the old Temple's destruction (586 BC) by fasting, since the new one was nearly completed. What the delegation really wanted to know was whether tradition was still relevant in changing times. The Lord answered them with a counter question: *"Was it really for me that you fasted?"* (v. 5). God did not say that fasting (tradition) was wrong, but enquired about the attitude behind it.

Whether or not the people fasted was not as important as whether they did it to honor God. It is so easy to do things just for the sake of tradition. "Tradition is a guide and not a jailer" (W. Somerset Maugham).

Prayer

Lord, I want to honor you in everything I do.

Today's Quote

Tradition is the living faith of those now departed. Traditionalism is the dead faith of those now living.
—Jaraslov Jan Pelikan

tradition

Asking Joel to tell the priest to get in touch with reality – and weep!

Bible passage

Joel 1 *Get in Touch with Reality – and Weep!*
13 And also you priests, put on your robes and join the outcry.
You who lead people in worship, lead them in lament. *(MSG)*

Devotion

Calamites like earthquakes, hurricanes, tornados, and droughts are devastating realities of life. We feel so powerless when it happens and sometimes wonder where God is in this. What can we, and especially the church, do when a calamity destroys lives and property? We could certainly do many things like sending money for relief efforts. But there is one thing that we all can, and should, do. The prophet Joel tells us what to do.

In the time of Joel a swarm of millions and millions of locusts have devastated the country of Judah. Every green thing has been stripped bare. The result is that famine is most certainly coming to the land. What are they going to do now?

Joel says to the priests, "put on your robes and join the outcry. You who lead people in worship, lead them in lament." This is no time for empty promises that everything will be okay. Rather, this is a time for pastors and other leaders to lead communities in weeping with those who weep. We can be so obsessed with our own happiness, so tuned in to the latest hits on iTunes and intrigued with the newest touch screens, that we become out of touch with the cry-Tunes of the world.

Prayer

God, help me to stay in touch with reality and cry with those who cry.

Today's Quote

Empty promises make for empty stomachs and that's literal.
—June Caldwell

Beautiful, More Beautiful, Esther

Bible passage

Esther 2 *Esther Made Queen*
17 Now the king was attracted to Esther more than to any of the other
women, and she won his favor and approval more than any of the other
virgins. So he set a royal crown on her head and made her queen instead
of Vashti. *(TNIV)*

Devotion

The story of Esther is remarkable, and yet the Lord is not mentioned in
the original text. Are the events in the story merely coincidental?

In Esther 1:1-22, the king's banquet ended in humiliation when Vashti,
the Persian king's wife, refused to be paraded before the men. The king's
advisors suggested that a beauty pageant be held to determine who
should be Vasthi's successor.

Esther was an orphan who was brought up by her cousin, Mordecai.
Esther was devastatingly beautiful. The king's agents noticed her and
entered her in the beauty pageant. They did not know that she was a Jew,
as Mordecai had forbidden her to reveal this fact out of fear that it might
count against her.

The organizers and the king were completely bowled over by Esther's
beauty. At a banquet, she was crowned as the queen who would replace
Vashti. It is remarkable to think that an orphan, a Jew, could be crowned
queen in a foreign country. Was this mere coincidence? No! God had
worked behind the scenes to make her queen. Likewise, God often works
in inconspicuous ways in our lives. All those coincidences in our lives
could be the result of God 's plan for our lives.

Prayer
Thank You, Lord, that You work mercifully in the shadows of my life.

Today's Quote
A coincidence is a small miracle in which God chooses to remain anonymous.
— Author unknown

coincidence?

Impressed with Mordecai who refused to kneel down to Haman. You should have seen Haman's face

Bible passage

Esther 3 *Haman's Plot to Destroy the Jews*
5 When Haman saw that Mordecai would not kneel down or pay him honor, he was enraged. *(TNIV)*

Devotion

You probably have a story to tell about the day your pride was hurt. It might have been the day when you were sworn at or when someone spread lies about you. It might have been the day the bank manager refused to give you a loan even though you had been a respected client for many years. It might have been the day your authority was disregarded and challenged. In the following episode, we read about the next main character in the book of Esther—a man whose pride was hurt.

In this episode, Haman is honored by the king and is given a position above all the other nobles in the kingdom. However, his pride was soon hurt when Mordecai refused to bow before him. Haman felt insulted and was furious (v. 5), and his anger soon turned to thoughts of revenge. When he heard that Mordecai was a Jew, he made plans to destroy all the Jews in the kingdom. By doing this, Haman became the Hitler in this story. Ironically, Haman's plans would cause his own downfall later on.

Thoughts of revenge bedevil relationships and make reconciliation impossible. Revenge targets the other person, but in the end we only end up destroying ourselves.

There is only one answer to revenge: Stop it!

Prayer
Lord, I confess that I often harbor thoughts of revenge against others.

Today's Quote
An eye for eye only ends up making the whole world blind.
—Mahatma Gandhi

March 12, 515 BC - What a glorious day!

Bible passage

Ezra 6: 13-18 *The Temple's Dedication*

14 So the elders of the Jews continued to build and prosper under the preaching of Haggai the prophet and Zechariah, a descendant of Iddo. They finished building the temple according to the command of the God of Israel ... [15] The temple was completed on the third day of the month Adar, in the sixth year of the reign of King Darius. *(TNIV)*

Devotion

How do you feel about history? Modern society does not always value history. We prefer to define ourselves in terms of where we are going, not where we come from. But history does matter. It has been said that he who controls the past controls the future. Our view of history shapes the way we view the present, and therefore it dictates what answers we offer for existing problems.

The Israelites realized the importance of history. The third day of the month of Adar in the sixth year of King Darius's rule is March 12, 515 BC on our calendar. On that day, after almost 21 years of construction, the Temple was finally completed. The prophets Haggai and Zechariah were thanked for their contribution. They had motivated the people to continue with the building of the Temple. It is interesting to note that the Persian kings Cyrus, Darius and Artaxerxes are also mentioned. They were sympathetic toward the building project and even provided the funding (vv. 6-12). Much like the Israelites, our lives are empty and lack substance if we do not value and celebrate our historical base.

Prayer

Thank You, Lord, for the wonderful historical base of Christianity.

Today's Quote

What is history? An echo of the past in the future; a reflex from the future on the
past

– Victor Hugo

Touched by Ezra's passionate prayer

Bible passage

Ezra 9 *Ezra's Prayer About Intermarriage*
6 "I am too ashamed and disgraced, my God, to lift up my face to you, because our sins are higher than our heads and our guilt has reached to the heavens. *(TNIV)*

Devotion

We all have a story about how someone disappointed us. It is part of life, but it is not always easy and pleasant to cope with. So how should we cope with it? We can learn a great deal from Ezra.

Ezra was a priest and scribe, who led the second group of exiles that returned from Babylon to Jerusalem. When Ezra arrived in Jerusalem, he discovered that the returned exiles had repeated the sins of their forefathers. They had married non-Jews and were worshipping their gods. Even the priests and the Levites were guilty of this. Ezra coped with this bad news in a very mature manner.

He showed his emotion. As a sign of grief and mourning, he tore his clothes and pulled out his beard (v. 5). Everyone noticed the dismay on his face. He then poured out these emotions to God in prayer. Ezra could have spoken very harshly to the Israelites, but instead he showed a lot of compassion for the people. Ezra did not use the words "you" or "they" when referring to the people in his prayer but rather "our" (v. 6). In this way, Ezra identified himself with the sins of his people.

The following quote by Martin Luther King Jr. sums up Ezra's attitude: "We must accept finite disappointment, but never lose infinite hope."

Prayer

Lord, help me to deal with the heartache in my life in a mature way.

Today's Quote

Disappointment to a noble soul is what cold water is to burning metal; it strengthens, tempers, intensifies, but never destroys it.
—Eliza Tabor

Hearing the cry of Nehemiah over the destruction of Jerusalem's Walls

Bible passage

Nehemiah 1 *Nehemiah's Concern for Jerusalem*

4 When I heard these things, I sat down and wept. For some days I mourned and fasted and prayed before the God of heaven. *(TNIV)*

Devotion

We don't need to feel embarrassed by tears. Charles Dickens said, "Heaven knows we need never be ashamed of our tears, for they are rain upon the blinding dust of earth, overlying our hard hearts." Voltaire said, "Tears are the silent language of grief." A Jewish proverb says: "What soap is to the body, tears are to the soul."

In this section, the tears that Nehemiah, the cupbearer to the Persian King, shed for his people can teach us something precious.

Nehemiah cried when he received the news about Jerusalem's broken walls. He did not ignore his pain but vented it in prayer and weeping. He took action and was in touch with his true feelings.

Tears can be very healing. Nehemiah's tears linked his pain to God's promises. In verse 8, he prays, "Remember the instruction you gave your servant Moses." His tears gave him courage to tackle the future. He decided to get up, wash his face and go and talk to the king (v. 11).

Through Nehemiah's example, we learn that we should also wrestle through the emotions caused by bad news because it leads to healing. Eventually you will experience the meaning of Nehemiah's name, "The Lord has comforted."

Prayer

Thank You, Lord that I can learn from Nehemiah that tears bring healing.

Today's Quote

Words that weep and tears that speak.
—Abraham Cowley

I wish people could have trusted Me more

Bible passage
Malachi 3: 10-15 *Don't Cheat God*

10 Bring the whole tithe into the storehouse, that there may be food in my house. Test me in this,' says the LORD Almighty, 'and see if I will not throw open the floodgates of heaven and pour out so much blessing that there will not be room enough to store it. *(TNIV)*

Devotion
The Bible is very clear that God wants to bless us. God's challenge to us is to trust Him for the blessing. Unfortunately, the Israelites didn't trust God in their difficult times. Drought and a plague of locust had tormented them. As a result, the people had withheld their tithes and offerings because they feared that their economic position would deteriorate even further. But the priests relied on these gifts for their livelihood. Consequently, the priests had nothing to eat (v. 10).

God wanted to teach the people to trust Him to bring their offerings even during tough times (v. 10). Of course, we should not see verse 10 as a business deal whereby we can buy prosperity from God. God challenged the Israelites (and us) to trust Him – even in tough times.

The things God wanted to use to bless them were not luxuries. Sufficient rain in the semi-desert in which they lived and pest-free harvests were crucial to their survival.

Even today, the Lord blesses us in many ways – like enough food, a car, a family. The problem is that we do not always see this as a blessing but as a matter of course. We often confuse blessings with luxuries. Perhaps we should make a list of all our blessings.

Prayer
Lord, I praise You for the many blessings that I receive daily.

Today's Quote
The proud man counts his newspaper clippings, the humble man his blessings.
— Fulton John Sheen

Time between the two Testaments
(± 400 – ± 6 BC)

The period between the Old – and New Testament is more than 400 years. Many things happened during that period.

▶ 333 BC: Alexander the Great conquered the Persians at the young age of 20 and established Greek rule throughout the land. The center of world power thus shifted from the east (Persia) to the west.

▶ 323-19 BC: The Egyptian Ptolemies, ancestors of Alexander's general, ruled over Palestine.

▶ 198-166 BC: Syrian Seleucids, ancestors of Alexander's general, ruled over Palestine.

▶ 166-63 BC: Judas Maccabees led a Jewish revolt and accomplished Jewish independence (166–63 B.C.). His ancestors, the Hasmoneans, ruled over Palestine for a century.

▶ 63 BC: Jerusalem falls at the hand of the Roman general, Pompey.

▶ 37 – 4 BC: The Romans appointed the rulers in Palestine themselves. One of the most unpopular choices among the Jews was probably the appointment of Herod as governor and later as king. The Jews saw this as a bitter pill, because Herod was a descendent of Esau (an Edomite) and his mother was of Arabic descent.

▶ Jewish resistance
Alexander the Great's attempts to Hellenize the world led to resistance, and new religious parties were formed among the Jews like the Pharisees, Sadducees and Zealots.

▶ Language
Latin was spoken in Rome, but *koine* Greek was spoken in the rest of the Roman Empire. The New Testament was written in Greek.

between the 2 testaments

The Life of Jesus – Tweets
(± 6BC – ± 27AD)
(Matthew, Mark, Luke and John)

▶ Jesus, a descendant of David, is born during the time of the Roman rule. At the age of approximately 30 years He was baptized by John and started his public ministry by teaching the people about the kingdom of God. He demonstrated the power of the kingdom of God by performing miracles.

▶ The religious leaders are upset about his claims of having a special relationship with God. Subsequently, they decided that He must be crucified.

▶ At the Last Supper (Passover meal) Jesus instituted the new covenant and promised his followers that they will receive a gift (Holy Spirit) to make this new covenant a reality.

▶ Jesus dies on the cross, rises from the dead and is seen by his followers. Before Jesus ascends to heaven, He tells his followers to go into the world to make people his disciples.

▶ The four Gospels describe the life of Jesus from different perspectives (Matthew, Mark, Luke and John).

I am light

Bible passage

Matthew 5 *The light of the world*

14 "You are the light of the world. A city on a hill can't be hidden. ¹⁵ Also, people do not light a lamp and put it under a bowl. Instead, they put it on its stand. Then it gives light to everyone in the house.

¹⁶ "In the same way, let your light shine in front of others. Then they will see the good things you do. And they will praise your Father who is in heaven. *(NIrV)*

Devotion

If God is light (1 John 1:5), how do you pray when you are experiencing dark times? Perhaps it would suffice to just pray, "Lord, please be my light!" But in what way is God the light?

The answer to the question, "In what way is God the light?" points to us, the believers. Jesus clearly says that we are the light of the world. How is this possible? The following story might help clarify this point.

A bomb destroyed a statue of Jesus that had been placed in front of a church during a war. When it fell, the hands and feet of the statue broke off. The church council decided to move the statue out of sight to the back of the church. They found it very difficult to have such a damaged statue of the Jesus figure in front of the church. However, after they had moved the statue, to their amazement they found the damaged statue back in its place in front of the church the next Sunday! An inscription was carved on the statue: "You are my hands and feet."

Prayer

Lord, forgive me for not always being Your hands and feet to other people. Help me to be the light of the world!

Today's Quote

There is not enough darkness in all the world to put out the light of even one small candle.

—Robert Alden

hands and feet

Watch out for greed

Bible passage

Matthew 6

22 Your eyes are like a window for your body. When they are good, you have all the light you need. 23 But when your eyes are bad, everything is dark. *(CEV)*

Devotion

Jesus talked about money more than anything else except the Kingdom of God. Why? Jesus realized that money so easily exercises power over us. Verses 22 and 23 will help us to understand how money exercises power over us. These two verses about the eye don't seem to fit Jesus' words about money (treasures 19-21 > eye < money 24vv). What does it do here?

The explanation of the eye is quite simple. If your eye is not working you cannot take the light in - your whole body will be in darkness although the room is flooded with light. You are probably wondering but what has this got to do with money? Verse 23 has the key – 'but if your eye is bad, everything is dark.' The Greek word for "dark" means greed. Jesus is saying: watch out for greed. Materialism has the peculiar effect to blind you spiritually, to distort the way you see things. Jesus did not say, "Watch out, you might be caught committing adultery" because you know when you commit adultery. But He needed to say, "Watch out, you might be greedy" because greed blinds you. Greed blinds you to ask questions about your lifestyle, how you make and spend your money.

How do we overcome greed? The key is in verse 22 – "When they are good." The Greek word for good is generous! Be generous!

Prayer

Lord, I realize anew that I am greedy. Help me to be generous!

Today's Quote

He who is greedy is always in want.

— Horace

Please don't judge others

Bible passage

Matthew 7: 1-6 *Be Fair When You Judge Others*
5 Hypocrite! First get rid of the log in your own eye; then you will see well enough to deal with the speck in your friend's eye. *(CEV)*

Devotion

The Bible has a lot to say about being judgmental. Jesus and the apostles understood clearly the human tendency to put down others.

Is it any surprise that most TV sitcoms are built around people tearing each other down, either behind their back or right to their face? It's terribly funny on TV - not at all funny in real life, especially if you are the person being degraded. Verse 5 comes as a strict warning not to judge other people, "Hypocrite! First get rid of the log in your own eye; then you will see well enough to deal with the speck in your friend's eye." The following story illustrates it very well.

A husband and wife's living room overlooked their new neighbor's backyard. One sunny morning the new neighbor hung out her laundry. The wife told her husband: "Look how dirty her laundry is. Doesn't she know how to wash laundry? Maybe she doesn't have laundry detergent. Poor thing!" It continued like that for several weeks.

One morning the husband's wife was totally amazed and said: "Look how clean is her laundry today! Maybe she got a new washing machine, or maybe she added detergent." "No," answered her husband. "I have cleaned the living room's windows early this morning."

Prayer

Merciful God, save me from hypocrisy. Teach us to be careful with each
other's feelings.

Today's Quote

*When we judge or criticize another person, it says nothing about that person; it
merely says something about our own need to be critical.*
— Author unknown

Unnecessary for Peter to fear but his walking on water was anyway awesome

Bible passage

Matthew 14: 25-33 *Jesus Walks on Water*

28 'Lord, is it you?' Peter asked. 'If it is, tell me to come to you on the water.' ²⁹ 'Come,' Jesus said. So Peter got out of the boat. He walked on the water toward Jesus. 30 But when Peter saw the wind, he was afraid. He began to sink. He cried out, 'Lord! Save me!' *(NIrV)*

Devotion

"Don't be afraid" is the most common instruction in the Bible — it occurs 366 times. A possible reason for this is that fear prevents us from getting out of the boat (our comfort zone). The only way to experience a fulfilled life is to take risks. We are afraid to swap the familiar for the unfamiliar. We have to choose between *fear* and *trust*. Fear tells us to *stay put* because we are comfortable where we are. Trust tells us to *move ahead* despite the risk involved. When failing becomes our greatest fear we become paralyzed, procrastinate, and see life as purposeless and boring.

How can you conquer your fear of failure? First, do not personalize failure. To sink does not turn you into a failure. Although Peter sank, Jesus called him a "rock" two chapters later (Matt. 16:18). Second, take action! You can't wait to be motivated — motivation is a byproduct of action. Action has a way of driving away fear. Finally, see failure as an opportunity to grow! Peter sank but found safety in the arms of Jesus.

If you don't make it your business to overcome fear, you better believe that it'll try to overcome you.

Prayer

Lord, I confess that my fears prevent me from following my calling. Help me!

Today's Quote

Fear defeats more people than any other one thing in the world.
— Ralph Waldo Emerson

To doubt is not as bad as you think

Bible passage

Matthew 28: 16-20 *The Great Commission*

17 When they saw him, they worshiped him. But some still had their doubts. [18] *Then Jesus came to them.* He said, 'All authority in heaven and on earth has been given to me. [19] So you must go and make disciples of all nations. *(NIrV)*

Devotion

How do we reconcile doubt with our faith? The last section of Matthew will shed some more light on doubt and faith.

Matthew 28:19-20 are well-known verses because they have become known as the "Great Commission." Because of this, we can easily read the chapter without paying attention to verses 16 to 18. Let us have a quick look at what these verses say. The first part of Matthew 28 is about the resurrection, followed by Jesus' encounter with the disciples. Verse 17 tells us that the disciples worshiped Jesus when they saw Him. But then the last part of the verse says, "But some still had their doubts." What was Jesus' reaction to the doubting disciples who left Him in the lurch at the cross?

The first few words of verse 18 express it so well: "Then Jesus came to them . . ." This is unbelievable. Jesus did not turn His back on the disciples or rebuke them because they doubted. Paul Tillich, a German-American theologian said, "Doubt isn't the opposite of faith; it is an element of faith." Doubt is the avenue through which we grow. When you doubt, you wrestle, question, and that just takes your faith to deeper levels. There is a proverb saying, "Doubt is the beginning, not the end of wisdom."

Prayer

Thank You, Lord, that You want to use me despite my doubt.

Today's Quote

Faith lives in honest doubt.
—Alfred, Lord Tennyson

Not married but I do have a Son

Bible passage

Mark 3: 7-12 *Crowds Follow Jesus*

11 When people with evil spirits saw him, they fell down in front of him. The spirits shouted, "You are the Son of God!" *(NIrV)*

Devotion

What does the Bible mean that Jesus is the "Son of God"? Does it mean that God has a wife or had sexual relations with Mary? That is not what the term means, nor is it what the Bible teaches, and it is not what Christianity teaches. The term "Son of God" refers not to procreation, but to a special relationship that Jesus has with God the Father.

For example, Arabs are generally known as the "sons of the desert," yet nobody believes that the desert physically gave birth to them. No, the name "sons of the desert" should be understood in a spiritual sense. Arabs are given that name because they have such a thorough knowledge of the desert; they are one with it. In the same way, when Mark writes that Jesus is the "Son of God," he emphasizes the intimate bond between Jesus and the Father.

In the biblical culture, Son of God was also a way to say that someone is equal to God, as John the Apostle stated "but he was even calling God his own Father, making himself equal with God" (John 5: 18 *NIV*).

The Apostle John also refers to Jesus as the Son of God to clearly indicate that Jesus, the Messiah, was indeed God (John 1:18). It is wonderful that God has made Himself known to us through Jesus.

Prayer

Lord, thank You that I know that You and the Father are one!

Today's Quote

You should point to the whole man *Jesus and say, "That is God."*
—Martin Luther

Woman's faith made Jesus' "No" to Crumble!

Bible passage

Mark 7: 24-30 *The Faith of a Gentile Woman*
27 'First let the children eat all they want,' he told her. 'It is not right to take the children's bread and throw it to their dogs.' ²⁸ 'Yes, Lord,' ... 'But even the dogs under the table eat the children's crumbs.' *(NIrV)*

Devotion

We all know the feeling of disappointment that we have when an urgent request is turned down with a firm *no*. The following story tells us about a woman who would not accept no from Jesus. Perhaps she could teach us something.

Jesus went to the non-Jewish area to rest. His rest was disturbed when a Greek woman begged Him to deliver her daughter from a demon. Jesus politely told her that He could not help her. His words in verse 27 confirm this: "It is not right to take the children's [Jews] bread and throw it to their dogs [non-Jews]."

The Jews often insulted the heathen (non-Jews) by calling them dogs because they believed that God did not bless heathens. In today's terms, the word "dog" would be the equivalent of "bitch." However, in this story, the dog was not at a loss for words. She uses Jesus' own words to challenge His no: "Lord, but even the dogs under the table eat the children's crumbs." By using these words, the woman admits that the Jews have the privilege to hear the gospel first, but insists that the Lord should also think about her. Her faith turned Jesus' no into a yes.   What was it about this foreigner that so moved the Master? It was her faith that challenged God!

Prayer

Thank You, Lord, that we can come to You with our requests.

Today's Quote

Faith makes all things possible.... love makes all things easy.
—Dwight L Moody

My Son's answer about taxes was awesome

Bible passage

Mark 12: 13-17 *Paying Taxes to Caesar*

14 They came to him and said, 'Teacher, we know you are a man of honor. You don't let others tell you what to do or say. You don't care how important they are. But you teach the way of God truthfully. Is it right to pay taxes to Caesar or not? [16] They brought the coin. He asked them, 'Whose picture is this? And whose words?' 'Caesar's,' they replied. [17] Then Jesus said to them, 'Give to Caesar what belongs to Caesar. And give to God what belongs to God.' They were amazed at him. *(NIrV)*

Devotion

Jesus' opponents tried to get rid of Him. They tried to achieve this by asking Him a tricky question. They did it very subtlety by first flattering Jesus (v. 14) in order to eliminate any suspicion He might have had about their motives and to force Him to answer them. The question about tax was exceptionally sly. If Jesus answered yes, the Jews would have turned against Him because they hated to pay taxes to the Romans. If He answered no, the Roman authority would have turned against Him.

Jesus answered their question by asking them a counter question: "Whose picture is this? And whose words?' 'Caesar's', they replied." The coin bore the image of Caesar, and therefore it belonged to the emperor. In a very clever way, Jesus lead them to realize that they also had to give to God that which bore God's image. What could that be? Our lives—because we were created in His image. Therefore, we belong to God! They were amazed at Him – so am I!

Prayer

Lord, my only comfort is that I know that I belong to You! Hallelujah!

Today's Quote

Behavior is the mirror in which everyone shows their image.

—Johann Wolfgang Von Goethe

Scribes learning not to mess with my Son

Bible passage
Mark 12: 28-34 *The Question about the Greatest Commandment*
30 Love the Lord your God with all your heart and with all your soul. Love him with all your mind and with all your strength.' [31] And here is the second one. 'Love your neighbor as you love yourself.' *(NIrV)*

Devoton
Many believers, especially children, often ask questions such as, "Is it wrong for a Christian to smoke, to visit night clubs, to have sex before marriage or to play the lotto?" Why do believers ask these questions? Perhaps they are afraid of God, or perhaps they want reassurance that the things they are doing are not really that bad. The Bible does not want us to function in this way.

In Jesus' time, the scribes were obsessed with what was wrong and what was right. This is why one of them asked Jesus to tell him what was the most important commandment. Jesus' answer showed him that there was something bigger than the commandments, namely love toward God and toward his neighbor. With this, Jesus wanted to show that religion was not about what should and what should not be done but about one's relationship with God and with one's neighbor.

My friend used the following theme for one of his sermons: "Is the lotto your motto?" Members of the congregation had the opportunity to air their views during the service. An old lady came up to my friend after the sermon and remarked, "Pastor, I do not play the lotto because my relationship with God is too important." My friend answered, "My dear, you don't know what an important thing you have just said."

Prayer
Lord, help me to do what is edifying for my relationship with You.

Devotion
You have a religion; I have a relationship.
— Anne Angelelli

relationship

Today is My 9/11

Bible passage

Mark 15: 33-37 *Jesus' death*

33 At the sixth hour darkness came over the whole land until the ninth hour. [34] And at the ninth hour Jesus cried out in a loud voice, "Eloi, Eloi, lama sabachthani?" — which means, "My God, my God, why have you forsaken me?"

[37] With a loud cry, Jesus breathed his last. *(NIV)*

Devotion

John Milton, an English poet, said, "Loneliness is about the scariest thing there is." Isn't that true? Even Jesus experienced excruciating loneliness. On that Friday afternoon that Jesus hung on the cross, His loneliness reached a low point. He was nailed to the cross, separated from everything and everyone — even from God. Then He cried out the words of Psalm 22: "My God, my God, why have you forsaken me?" *(NIV)*.

Yet this agonizing cry was already filled with triumph. It was uttered at the end of the three hours of darkness, when Jesus' work was done. Satan wanted Jesus to go one step further — He wanted Jesus to forsake the Father. During those three hours, the darkness must have tempted Him to repeatedly swear at God and die. Hell expected Jesus to swear, but instead it got the words from the Psalm!

Although God had left Him, Jesus did not turn His back on His Father. Because Jesus called out in bewilderment during that hour, "My God, my God, why have you forsaken me?" we can now call out in wonder, "My God, my God why did You adopt me?" The Father left His own Son to ensure that you and I will never be forsaken.

Prayer

The Lord is my shepherd. He gives me everything I need.

Today's Quote

Loneliness is the most terrible poverty.

— Mother Teresa of Calcutta

Pleased to see My Son baptized

Bible passage

Luke 3: 21-22 *Jesus' Baptism*

21 One day when the crowds were being baptized, Jesus himself was baptized. As he was praying, the heavens opened, [22] and the Holy Spirit, in bodily form, descended on him like a dove. And a voice from heaven said, "You are my dearly loved Son, and you bring me great joy." *(CEV)*

Devotion

It's interesting that people often use slogans on their T-shirts to convey messages. Just the other day, I read a message on the back of someone's T-shirt that said, "Guess what? Nobody cares!"

In the time of Jesus, John the Baptist was baptizing people who repented of their sins. Baptism was therefore a sign of repentance. So, if this was the case, why did Jesus want to be baptized? After all, He was without sin. By being baptized, Jesus was identifying fully with us—especially with those who confess their sins. Further proof of His identification with human beings is that He was baptized with other people.

The heavens opened, the Holy Spirit descended like a dove upon Jesus. while the Father called from heaven, "You are my dearly loved Son, and you bring me great joy." This gave Jesus divine authority. The involvement of the Holy Spirit and the Father is further proof that God identifies Himself with human beings. This is what makes God so laudable. He became part of our history—our world. He really cares! May your life be a witness to change the T-shirt's " nobody" to a "somebody."

Prayer

Thank You, Lord, that You care for me by truly identifying with me.

Today's Quote

I don't care how much you know until I know how much you care.
— Author unknown

Jesus became very busy. I am so glad He took a break

Bible passage

Luke 5: 12-16 *A Leper Comes to Jesus*

13 Jesus reached out his hand and touched the man. 'I am willing to do it,' he said. 'Be 'clean'!' Right away the disease left him. ¹⁶ But Jesus would often go to some place where he could be alone and pray. *(NIrV)*

Devotion

The standard answer nowadays when asked, "How are you?" is "Busy." Jesus was also busy but He never neglected quiet time.

Jesus changed many people's lives radically. In this passage, He gave a leper new hope by curing him. In those days, lepers were social outcasts. Nobody touched them. They were unable to work and had no income to support their families, and they could not attend religious assemblies. They were completely isolated from society and their friends. In our day, this could be compared to having AIDS.

Many people flocked to Jesus to listen to Him and to be cured by Him. His popularity increased and His days were busy. Jesus realized that He could not keep this schedule up. So He did what we often neglect to do—He went to a secluded spot to pray.

Prayer and quiet time will help you to focus on God, and it is a vital source of strength. When things sometimes overwhelm you, the best thing to do is to become quiet in prayer. If Jesus needed to do this, just imagine how much you need to do this from time to time.

Prayer

Thank you, Lord, that in Your presence I am able to experience quiet time in any place.

Today's Quote

To be a Christian without prayer is no more possible than to be alive without breathing.
—Martin Luther King, Jr.

Telling someone, in a polite way, that he is a fool

Bible passage

Luke 12: 13-21 *Parable of the Rich Fool*

15 Then he said to them, 'Watch out! Be on your guard against wanting to have more and more things. Life is not made up of how much a person has.'

Tension: (vv. 16-17) The rich man's harvest is too large for his barn.

Relief of Tension: (vv. 18-19) He builds bigger barns.

Result: (vv. 20-21) God thinks he is a fool. *(NIrV)*

Devotion

I once asked a friend of mine what he would like his life to look like in 10 year's time. His answer was short and sweet: "I want to be retired and on every golf course in the world." This section in Luke also describes dreams of eating, drinking and living the good life.

This successful man in Jesus' parable enlarged his barns and pursued his dreams. This was very noble, yet God considered him a fool. Why? There are three distinct reasons why God called him a fool: He was selfish, as he constantly referred to "my" and "I." He thought he had control of his life, but when God demanded his life (v. 20), he discovered that he merely had control over his belongings. He wanted to organize his own life—but without God. The words in verse 18 ("This is what I'll do") and those in verse 19 ("I'll say to myself") are proof of this.

It is not wrong to have goals; God just wants us to have the right attitude and not be greedy. Life is not made up of how much a person has (v. 15), but rather, how much are you willing to share.

Prayer

Lord, help me to have the correct attitude toward money and wealth.

Today's Quote

Complete possession is proved only by giving. All you are unable to give possesses you.
— Andre Gide

You gotta read this. It is the best short story ever

Bible passage

Luke 15: 11-32 *Parable of the Lost Son*
18 I will get up and go back to my father. I will say to him, 'Father, I have sinned against heaven. And I have sinned against you. *(NIrV)*

Devotion

Many consider the parable of the lost (prodigal) son as the best short story ever told. Jesus tells this parable after the Pharisees and religious leaders accuse him of welcoming and eating with "sinners.

The parable begins with a young man (represents sinners), the younger of two sons, who asks his father (represents God) to give him his share of the estate. The parable continues by describing how the younger son travels to a distant country on a self-discovery mission. He lost all his money in wild living. He lost all his values because he practiced free sex. He lost all his dignity because a Jew who looked after pigs was condemned by his fellow countrymen. His urge to eat the food of pigs was the lowest point to which a Jew could stoop. Furthermore, he also lost his right and claim to be acknowledged as a son.

The young man had bumped his head very hard. But there was one thing he could not lose—his father's love. This time, the young man did not long for what was in his father's hand but what was in his father's heart. The story's turning point is in verse 17, when he came to his senses. He decided to confess his sins to his father and to God. His father welcomed him back and threw a huge party. This parable tells us that God will always forgive you – no matter what you have done. Jesus wanted to tell the Pharisees that Jesus loves sinners (but not sin).

Prayer

Lord, help me to be honest in confessing my sins to You and to others.

Today's Quote

The confession of evil works is the first beginning of good works.
—Saint Augustine

If something sounds too good to be true, it probably is – but not in this case

Bible passage

Luke 15: 11-32 *Parable of the Lost Son*
20 'While the son was still a long way off, his father saw him. He was filled with tender love for his son. He ran to him. He threw his arms around him and kissed him. *(NIrV)*

Devotion

The youngest son, who messed up, must have returned home with a fearful heart, wondering: *What will my father say?* Yet it is interesting to note that the father did five things before he even said *anything* to him. According to verse 20, these five reactions were:

1. He saw his son while he was still a long way off—which means that he had waited for him all the time!

2. He pitied him deeply—his eyes were not filled with anger but with tears.

3. He ran to meet him—he took the initiative.

4. He embraced him—the prodigal son experienced unconditional love.

5. He kissed him—this was considered undignified conduct for an Oriental father, but it did not bother him to act in this way because the news about his son's return was overwhelming.

In this manner, the father eased his son's final steps on his return. When his son expressed remorse (v. 21), the father did not answer directly but arranged a feast for him. The father's actions indicated that he had forgiven his son. God is the father who always rejoices when someone who went astray returns home, shows remorse and confesses.

Prayer
Lord, I want to praise You for showing me so much mercy.

Today's Quote
Every saint has a past and every sinner has a future.
—Oscar Wilde

Not about good or bad but about humility or pride

Bible passage

Luke 15: 11-32 *Parable of the Lost Son*

32 "But we had to celebrate and be glad, because this brother of yours was dead and is alive again; he was lost and is found." *(NIrV)*

Devotion

The eldest son's bitter reaction stood in stark contrast to his father's joy. The eldest son felt that his younger brother did not deserve the festivities, because he had squandered all his money on prostitutes. He was bitter because he had been a loyal son all those years and yet did not receive festive recognition for it.

Jesus wants to show the Pharisees (the audience) that they are lost, not in spite of their goodness but because of their goodness. They use their goodness as self-justification. The eldest son uses moral conformity (goodness) to get to his father's wealth and status. The youngest son (sinners) uses self-discovery (sins) to get to his father's stuff. Both sons are lost. The youngest son is lost in his lostness and the elder son is lost in is goodness. Self-discovery and moral conformity can never save you. It doesn't go deep enough to take you to the father's heart. How can we be saved?

1. We need the initiating love of the Father (Luke 15: 20, 28)
2. We need to repent of our sins as well as the wrong reasons why we do good.
3. We need to be melted and moved at what it costs the Father to bring us back home.

Prayer

Lord, I want to show by my way of living that I love You.

Today's Quote

Hurt leads to bitterness, bitterness to anger, travel too far that road and the way is lost.

— Terry Brooks

If My Son, Jesus, is the answer, what is the question?

Bible passage

John 7 *Jesus Promises Living Water*

37 Jesus stood up and cried out, 'If anyone thirsts, let him come to me and drink. [38] Whoever believes in me, as the Scripture has said, 'Out of his heart will flow rivers of living water." *(ESV)*

Devotion

Many people want to turn Jesus into a formula. Just think of the graffiti and bumper stickers that say: "Jesus is the answer!" Someone once asked, "But what is the question?" Let us say that the question is: "Who / what quenches my thirst?"

A living relationship with Jesus is not enough to quench life's thirst. Now, before you object that this point of view is too risky, consider the example of Adam. Initially, he had a perfect relationship with God, but he still thirsted for a companion. God noticed this yearning and gave him a wife.

Thirst is a concept that involves God and other people. If we want to quench our thirst only with God, we will lose out on people. Likewise, if we want to quench our thirst only with people, we will lose out with God. We all have different kinds of thirsts. Our thirst might lie in unanswered questions such as: What is the meaning of life? Why did my relationship fail? Why do I have to endure so much pain? The answers to these questions do not lie in a formula but in a promise: "Out of his heart will flow rivers of living water" (v. 38).

Prayer

Thank You, God, that Your promise will meet my thirst.

Today's Quote

Love shortens time, changes the hours. Love is invincible. Many waters cannot quench it nor the floods drown. The supreme happiness of life is the conviction that we are loved.

— Author unknown

Will never forget the shame in the eyes of this woman

Bible passage
John 8: 1-11 A Woman Caught in Adultery
6 They were trying to trap him into saying something they could use against him, but Jesus stooped down and wrote in the dust with his finger. *(NLT)*

Devotion
This is one of the most dramatic episodes in the whole life of Jesus when the Pharisees and Scribes brought to Jesus a woman whom they had caught in the act of adultery.

Jesus knew that their intention was to trap Him. If Jesus would approve her stoning, He would become a criminal in the eyes of the Roman government because Jews had no right to pass the death sentence. If Jesus would disapprove, it would immediately be said that He was teaching people to break the Law. What a dilemma!

Jesus did not to answer their question at all, but stooped over and started to write on the ground with his finger. Maybe He wanted to gain time and not to be rushed into a decision. We don't know what He wrote. Someone said that He probably wrote: Where is the man?

The Pharisees demanded an answer and the answer they got was drenched with divine wisdom: "*If any one of you is without sin, let him be the first to throw a stone at her.*" All you could hear was probably doef, doef as they dropped the stones and drifted away.

Jesus did not blast her, but inspired her with the challenge: "Go now and leave your life of sin."

Prayer
God, I thank You that You are a kind and loving God who loves us!

Today's Quote
Our chief want is someone who will inspire us to be what we know we could be.
— Ralph Waldo Emerson

Please don't treat My Spirit as a stepchild of your faith

Bible passage

John 14: 15-31 *Jesus promises the Holy Spirit*
16 Then I will ask the Father to send you the Holy Spirit who will help you and always be with you. [18] I won't leave you like orphans. I will come back to you. *(CEV)*

Devotion

The Holy Spirit is often treated as the stepchild of faith. Perhaps this is because the word "Spirit" conjures up something spooky, or perhaps it is because a lot of people see the Spirit as a vague and impersonal force.

The Bible makes it clear that the Holy Spirit is not a vague and impersonal force. The Holy Spirit is a personal being who is equal to God the Father and God the Son. According to the Bible, the Holy Spirit has an intellect (1 Cor 2:11), emotions (Rom 15:30) and a will (1 Cor 12:11).

Jesus said that it was to our advantage that He had to leave (John 16: 7). Why would He say this? His life, His death and His resurrection made many things possible for us. For instance, Jesus made it possible for us to know the Father; to forgive; to experience love, joy and peace; to be patient, friendly, kind-hearted, faithful and humble; and to apply self-constraint. He sent His Spirit to live within us and to turn all these possibilities into realities. The Spirit does it by guiding us into the full truth (John 16: 13).

We, therefore, need to be filled with the Holy Spirit (Ephesians 5: 18). To be filled with the Holy Spirit is a daily process whereby we commit ourselves anew to Christ and His Word. We, therefore, cannot treat the Holy Spirit as a stepchild of our faith.

Prayer
Thank You, Lord, for sending your Spirit to guide us.

Today's Quote
The Holy Spirit turns that which Jesus made possible into a reality.

Witnessing something remarkable

Bible passage

John 19: 23-27 *The Crucifixion*

26 When Jesus saw his mother and his favorite disciple with her, he said to his mother, 'This man is now your son.' [27] Then he said to the disciple, 'She is now your mother.' From then on, that disciple took her into his own home. *(CEV)*

Devotion

Mother Teresa said, "The most terrible poverty is loneliness, and the feeling of being unloved." Isn't that true? The unfortunate reality is that our society is filled with lonely people. On the Friday that Jesus was crucified, something remarkable happened that teaches us something about Jesus and loneliness.

On that Friday, Jesus was probably the loneliest person on earth. He experienced complete separation from God and helplessly watched as His last belongings, His clothes, were divided among four soldiers. Jesus' pain and loneliness intensified when He saw that only His mother, three other women, and John attended the crucifixion. The other disciples had become filled with fear and had run away.

Although Jesus experienced enormous pain and loneliness, He brought people together when He told John, "She is now your mother" (v. 27). It is remarkable that, despite His own suffering, Jesus was able to bring people together so that they could care for each other and escape loneliness. Jesus experienced separation from God so that we need never be without God and each other. There are many things you could do not to be lonely – like volunteer or join a small group.

Prayer

Lord, help me to reach out to those who are lonely.

Today's Quote

The eternal quest of the human being is to shatter his loneliness.
— Norman Cousins

My Son's last dying words

Bible passage
John 19: 28-30 *The Death of Jesus*
30 When he had received the drink, Jesus said, "It is finished." With that, he bowed his head and gave up his spirit. *(NIV)*

Devotion
We should be grateful that so many famous people's dying words have been recorded, as their words reveal so much. Here is a couple:

Alexander the Great: "There are no more other worlds to conquer!"

James Dean: "My fun days are over."

Fortunately, we also have a record of Jesus' last words before he died: "It is finished." In Greek it is one word, "tetelestai."

When Jesus died He did not say, "I am finished," for that would imply that He died defeated and exhausted. "It is finished" means that Jesus accomplished everything that he was supposed to do.

He came to pay a debt He didn't owe because we owed a debt we couldn't pay. A debtor (sinner) cannot pay another debtor's debt. It is like a criminal who cannot be a defense lawyer for another criminal. We were toast. We were unable to make up for sin. The debt of sin is eternal death and we were not able to overcome death.

There was no human being who was able to pay our debt. That is why God became flesh in Jesus, the sinless human being, to pay our debt with His sinless blood. Tetelestai was also a legal term in those days, to indicate when an account was paid in full. So, when God looks at our bill, all He sees is the stamp, in blood, "Paid in full." Halleluja!

Prayer
Thank You, Jesus, that Your death has made me debt free. Wow!

Today's Quote
He came to pay a debt He didn't owe because we owed a debt we couldn't pay.
— Author unknown

The early Church – Tweets
(± 27AD – ± 100AD)

▶ Jesus' followers receive the gift of God, the Holy Spirit, who gives them a new experience of God's presence and power.

▶ Christian communities are being formed and grow with the spreading of the Good News. The church exists of different cultures and nationalities.

▶ The authors of the gospel (Matthew, Mark, Luke and John) tell the narrative of the life and ministry of Jesus. The letters of the New Testament are written by church leaders to help people understand how their faith influences their daily life and hope for the future.

▶ The books about the early church can be divided as follow:
- The Acts of the Apostles, which describes the first years of the Christian Church
- The letters of Paul (Romans, 1 and 2 Corinthians, Galatians, Ephesians, Philippians, Colossians, 1 and 2 Thessalonians, 1 and 2 Timothy, Titus and Philemon)
- The general letters (Hebrews, James, 1 and 2 Peter, 1–3 John and Jude)
- John's visions (Revelation)

My Spirit will give you what you need

Bible passage

Acts 1: 1-8 *The Promise of the Holy Spirit*
8 But you will receive power when the Holy Spirit has come upon you, and you will be my witnesses in Jerusalem and in all Judea and Samaria, and to the end of the earth.' *(ESV)*

Devotion

Christians continue Christ's work by being witnesses. But in actual fact, many of us are afraid to bear witness. One of the main reasons is that we do not always know how the other person will react—we might be rejected. To overcome these fears, we need the power of the Holy Spirit.

The power of the Holy Spirit is more than just the supernatural and the extraordinary workings of the Spirit. The power of the Spirit also means that one has the courage, fearlessness, insight and wisdom to testify with style.

One day St. Francis of Assisi invited a young monk to join him on a trip into town to preach. The young monk was so honored that he quickly accepted. All day long they walked through the streets, and rubbed shoulders and visited with hundreds of people. At the end of the day they headed back home; however, not even once had St. Francis talked to anyone about the gospel. The young monk was disappointed, and said to St. Francis, "I thought we were going into town to preach?" St. Francis responded, "My son, we have preached. We were preaching while we were walking. We were seen by many and our behavior was closely watched. It is of no use to walk anywhere to preach unless we preach everywhere as we walk!" Our lives speak louder than words.

Prayer

Lord, I realize anew what responsibility I have to live the right life.

Today's Quote

Preach the Gospel at all times, and if necessary, sometimes use words.
—St. Francis of Assisi

What "Good" People Also Need!

Bible passage

Acts 9: 1-20 *Saul's Conversion*
3 When Saul had almost reached Damascus, a bright light from heaven suddenly flashed around him. [4] He fell to the ground and heard a voice that said, 'Saul! Saul! Why are you so cruel to me?' *(CEV)*

Devotion

We all know this story. It is a story of conversion — perhaps the best known one of all. It is the story of an archenemy of the Church who became a brother — Saul, who became Paul! Even today, many Christians use Paul's conversion as the model for their own story — stories such as, "I was wild, bad and sinful. Then I had a Damascus Road experience — the Lord intervened and I was made new! I was addicted, but now I am free."

These stories are gripping. But we should realize that Paul was not a wild or bad person. He was a "good" person. Yet after his Damascus experience, he makes the following remark about his good virtues: "But Christ has shown me that what I once thought was valuable is worthless. Nothing is as wonderful as knowing Christ Jesus my Lord. I have given up everything else and count it all as garbage. All I want is Christ" (Phil. 3:7-8, *CEV*).

The reality is that you might consider yourself as good person comparing to crooks and criminals but comparing to God we all fall short to the glory of God (Rom 3: 23). For this reason, "good" people also need to be converted to the One who washed away all our iniquity and cleansed us from our sin (Ps 51: 2).

Prayer
Create in me a pure heart, O God,
and renew a steadfast spirit within me. (Ps 51: 10 *NIV*).

Today's Quote
The question isn't were you challenged. The question is were you changed?
— Leonard Ravenhill

So impressed with the businesswoman of Philippi

Bible passage

Acts 16: 11-15 *Lydia's Conversion in Philippi*
15 Then after she and her family were baptized, she kept on begging us,
'If you think I really do have faith in the Lord, come stay in my home.'
Finally, we accepted her invitation. *(CEV)*

Devotion

The Bible places a high value on hospitality (Rom 12: 13). Hospitality
means, "love of strangers." To be new in a neighborhood, a school, or
alone at a party can be very challenging.

Paul and his friends also felt like strangers on their first outreach to
Europe. In the city of Philippi (northern Greece) Lydia, a trader in
expensive purple woolen cloth, became the first convert of Europe. After
her conversion, she immediately showed hospitality towards Paul and
his friends by begging them to stay over at her house.

Even businesses understand the importance of hospitality. Danny
Meyer is one of the most famous restaurateurs in New York City. He
attributes his success not just to the quality of the food, but to the
attention he places on hospitality. His book's title, "Setting the Table: The
Transforming Power of Hospitality in Business", speaks for itself.

Danny says everyone wants great service. However, there is a
difference between service—someone doing what they're supposed to
do—versus hospitality. According to Danny, service doesn't say anything
about how someone made you feel. Hospitality does.

Prayer

Lord, I want to be more aware of the opportunities to show hospitality.

Today's Quote

I've learned that people will forget what you said, people will forget what you
did, but people will never forget how you made them feel.
—Maya Angelou

What is so amazing about grace?

Bible passage
Romans 3 *Undeserved kindness*
23 for all have sinned and fall short of the glory of God, 24 and are justified freely by his grace through the redemption that came by Christ Jesus. *(NIV)*

Devotion
The apostle Paul loves to use the word grace. But what is so amazing about grace?

Philip Yancey tells this story of C.S. Lewis. During a British conference on comparative religions, experts from around the world debated what, if any, belief was unique to the Christian faith. They began eliminating possibilities. Incarnation? Other religions had different versions of gods appearing in human form. Resurrection? Again, other religions had accounts of return from death. The debate went on for some time until C. S. Lewis wandered into the room. "What's the rumpus about?" he asked, and heard in reply that his colleagues were discussing Christianity's unique contribution among world religions. Lewis responded, "Oh, that's easy. It's grace."

After some discussion, the conferees had to agree. The notion of God's love coming to us free of charge, no strings attached, seems to go against every instinct of humanity. The Buddhist eight-fold path, the Hindu doctrine of karma, the Jewish covenant, and the Muslim code of law -- each of these offers a way to earn approval. Only Christianity dares to make God's love unconditional. (from What is so amazing about grace? page 45)

Prayer
God, I thank You for undeserved kindness shown to me.

Today's Quote
Grace is given to heal the spiritually sick, not to decorate spiritual heroes.
—Martin Luther

Something a government cannot conquer

Bible passage

Romans 13 *Submission to the Authorities*

1 Obey the rulers who have authority over you. Only God can give authority to anyone, *(CEV)*

Devotion

How do you feel about your government? The apostle Paul writes very positively about governments. He tells us that we should submit ourselves to our governing authorities. Before we set about criticizing Paul, we should briefly consider why Paul made this request.

Although Jesus died and rose again and there is now a Church on earth, sin still prevails. For this reason, God established authorities (v. 1) to prevent things from getting out of hand. The laws of government that instill fear in people prevent society from deteriorating into chaos. Governments can never conquer the evil in people, but they can prevent it from erupting into violence and chaos.

The Church cannot fulfill this function, because it has not been called to keep people in check through authority and power. Instead, the Church has been called to conquer evil through good. This means that a believer's behavior is motivated from the inside by means of love, and not from the outside by means of punishment and fear for authority. Fear says "I have to," while love says, "I want to."

We should keep on praying for the authorities to perform their duties and responsibilities to the benefit of us all.

Prayer

Lord, enable me through Your Holy Spirit to conquer evil with good.

Today's Quote

The church must be reminded that it is not the master or the servant of the state, but rather the conscience of the state. It must be the guide and the critic of the state, and never its tool.

—Martin Luther King, Jr.

from the inside

It is just fine if Christians have differences

Bible passage

Romans 14 *The Danger of Criticism*

3 People who eat everything must not look down on those who do not. And people who don't eat everything must not judge those who do. God has accepted them. *(NIrV)*

Devotion

It is sad when Christians fight among themselves—usually about trivial matters! In Paul's day, the believers differed among themselves on what food was pure and what food was impure. Some believers only ate vegetables, because they considered all other food impure. According to these believers, the other Christians were committing sin by eating the so-called impure food. Paul referred to these believers as weak (verse 2), because they did not realize that they were free and could eat any food they wished.

Although Paul spoke to both groups, he agreed with the strong ones. He asked them to accept the weak ones and not to despise them. The strong ones could win the argument that all food was pure but could lose the person. Paul also instructed the weak believers, who considered all kinds of things sinful, not to judge the believers who differed from them in their beliefs.

Paul based his explanation on a wonderful comment: "God has accepted them." Even today, believers have different opinions on moral issues (such as abortion and homosexuality) and dogmatic issues (such as baptism). Let's learn to accept one another and not condemn and labeled each other . . . because God has accepted us!

Prayer

Lord, help me not to look down on others or to judge others.

Today's Quote

In essentials, unity; in differences, liberty; in all things, charity.
— Philipp Melanchthon

Understand that following Me sounds foolish

Bible passage

1 Corinthians 1: 18-25 *God's wisdom*

23 But we preach that Christ was nailed to a cross. Most Jews have problems with this, and most Gentiles think it is foolish. *(CEV)*

Devotion

Just the other day, someone told me nonchalantly that he was not a churchgoer. Speaking to him made me realize that more and more, Christianity doesn't appeal to people. In fact, it often pushes people away! Paul understood only too well why people consider Christianity nonsense. Let us call it godly nonsense!

The Jews and the Greeks (gentiles) regarded the message of the cross as nonsense. The Jews expected a Messiah who would act with power and authority. They therefore considered it repulsive that someone whose life ended shamefully on a cross could be the Son of God. The Greeks believed that it was an insult to God to get involved in human matters. They believed that God was *apathetic* and devoid of emotion. If God were to show any emotion, it would mean that the behavior of human beings could influence Him. Therefore, the message of the cross, which demonstrated God's passion for people, made no sense to them.

However, this godly nonsense contains more wisdom than the wisdom of human beings. It shows that God's supposed weakness (His death on the cross) was greater than the power of human beings (1 Cor. 1:25). God showed this by using His love to turn a cross—a symbol of hate—into a symbol of hope. With time, human beings discovered that this godly nonsense was the only way to real happiness.

Prayer

Thank You, Lord for turning the cross into a symbol of hope.

Today's Quote

The name of Jesus is the one lever that lifts the world.
— Author Unknown

godly nonsense

Faith, Hope and Love are like triplets

Bible passage

1 Corinthians 13 *Love is the greatest*

13 And now these three remain: faith, hope and love. But the greatest of these is love. *(NIV)*

Devotion

Three words describe the Christian life: faith, hope and love. Paul liked to write about these three important issues and always related them to each other. Let us see what they have in common.

Love is God's invitation to the world to have faith in Him and to follow Him, the origin of life. Christian faith is not merely a religious conviction but also an act of love. Faith and love are therefore the two pillars of the Christian life. These two pillars are built on the foundation of hope.

In colloquial language, "hope" means "maybe" — you hope it will rain next week, but you are not sure. Biblical hope, however, means "definitely." Hope directs faith and love to our future in heaven — something that is fixed and certain.

Hope is like a pair of binoculars that brings that which is far away (eternal life) closer. This helps us to gain perspective on the here and now. Hope fuels faith and love. It drives faith and inspires love.

To sum up: *faith* gives *love* and *hope* substance — Jesus Christ.

Love gives *faith* and *hope* a heart — the love of Jesus Christ.

Hope gives *faith* and *love* a future — eternal life.

Prayer

Thank You, Lord, that I can live in faith, hope and love!

Today's Quote

Nothing worth doing is completed in our lifetime; therefore we must be saved by hope. Nothing true or beautiful makes complete sense in any immediate context of history; therefore we must be saved by faith. Nothing we do, however virtuous, can be accomplished alone; therefore, we are saved by love.

— Reinhold Niebuhr

Like this graffiti

Bible passage

1 Corinthians 15 *Death has no more sting*
56 Sin is what gives death its sting,
and the Law is the power behind sin. *(CEV)*

Devotion

The entire chapter of 1 Corinthians 15 deals with the question of whether there is life after death. In this chapter, Paul compares death to a bee with a dangerous sting—the sting of sin. God allowed the "bee of death" to pierce Jesus (and not us) on the cross with its sting of *sin*, thereby causing His death. However, when Jesus was resurrected from the grave, the bee of death was conquered and lost its poisonous sting of sin (v. 57). Our relationship of faith with Jesus enables us to share in this victory. We should thank God for this (v. 57).

Although we might at times feel that being a Christian is all in vain (v. 58), the fact that there is life after death makes it worth our while to persevere. We should, however, not content ourselves with the question of whether there is life after death. The following graffiti was once seen on a wall: "Is there life after death?" Someone then came and wrote the following beneath it: "Is there life before death?" Considering all the hurt and sorrow of life, this is a very significant question. Sometimes we worry so much about life after death that we battle to live a meaningful life on this side of the grave. Paul, therefore, warns us to stand firm and to give ourselves fully to God's work (v. 58). We, therefore, have the responsibility to convince humankind that we can live completely before death.

Prayer

Lord, thank You that you made life after death possible.

Today's Quote

If I think more about death than some other people, it is probably because I love life more than they do.
— Angelina Jolie

Will always comfort you in troubled times

Bible passage

2 Corinthians 1 *God Offers Comfort to All*
3 Praise God, the …! The Father is a *merciful* God, who always gives us *comfort.* [4] He *comforts* us when we are in trouble, so that we can share that same *comfort* with others in trouble. [5] We share in the terrible sufferings of Christ, but also in the wonderful *comfort* he gives. *(CEV)*

Devotion

Life, with all its sharp edges, has a way of getting us down. From time to time, despondency bowls us over. During such times, we need something specific to help us carry on with life. Paul writes about this in the following section.

Paul experienced great difficulties as a missionary, but he did not seek sympathy in his letter to the Corinthians. Instead, He thanked God. Paul looked back and realized that God had compassion on him and saved him from every difficult situation (v. 3). He compared the comfort he enjoyed to a relay stick that had to be passed on to those who, like him, experienced difficulties (v. 4).

Difficult times are just a part of life, and during such times the saddened heart seeks comfort. Paul felt so strongly about this that he used the word "comfort" four times in the above three verses. The question is how we can pass on the relay stick of comfort. We can do this by simply showing sincere interest in someone who is in need and by listening to that person before giving answers or making comments prematurely. Let us pass that which we receive from God and others on to each other: the relay stick of comfort!

Prayer

Lord, help me to pass on the comfort I receive to others.

Today's Quote

God can heal a broken heart, but He has to have all the pieces.
— Author Unknown

Just Love it when someone gives cheerfully

Bible passage

2 Corinthians 9 *Giving Generously*

6 The point is this: whoever sows sparingly will also reap sparingly, and whoever sows bountifully will also reap bountifully. ⁷ Each one must give as he has made up his mind, not reluctantly or under compulsion, for God loves a *cheerful giver*. *(ESV)*

Devotion

Christians differ on giving tithes. Should it be a full tenth? Those who say yes differ on whether it should be a tenth of gross income or net income. Some argue that the tithe is a law of the Old Testament and no longer applies to Christians. This section will shed some light on this important issue.

Paul does not ask money for the church's building project or to balance the books. (In those days, "church" referred to a movement rather than to expensive structures.) Instead, he asks for money for the believers in Judea. He does not prescribe how much they should give, but gives a general *guideline* (v. 6). He uses an example from nature of sowing seed. The more seed you sow, the more you will reap. Of course, this might not be in material things but in treasures of the heart—you will become richer in love, friends, helpfulness and peace with God. You never lose your harvest when you sow in the fields of people's needs.

Paul also states that it is important to have the right *attitude* when you give. God loves a cheerful giver (v. 7). Nobody can prescribe how much you should give; the amount should stem from your heart.

Prayer

Thank You, Lord, for the privilege to give and to receive.

Today's Quote

Never measure your generosity by what you give,
but rather by what you have left.
—Bishop Fulton J. Sheen

Like the way Paul explains Jesus and the Law

Bible passage

Galatians 4 *Jesus and the Law*

4 But when the time was right, God sent his Son, and a woman gave birth to him. His Son obeyed the Law, [5] so he could set us free from the Law, and we could become God's children. *(CEV)*

Devotion

Paul's whole purpose for the book of Galatians was to convince the believers that they were not saved because they obeyed the Law but because they had faith. Yet despite this, Jesus had to submit Himself to the Law. Why did Jesus have to do this, but we do not?

Paul uses the example of a minor to explain spiritual immaturity. A minor could only inherit from his father on the day that his father determined he would be mature. The minor's age stood in his way.

Similarly, the Law stands in the way preventing human beings from inheriting eternal life. The Law keeps us spiritually immature because we constantly stumble over the demands (obedience) of the Law. Stumbling (disobedience) means that the punishment of the Law, eternal death, awaits us — which means we inherit nothing.

However, when Jesus became human and submitted to the Law, He did not falter. As a perfect human being, Jesus could meet the demands of the Law. He conquered the consequence of our stumbling — namely, eternal death — on the cross. Believing in Him enables us to share in this triumph and inherit eternal life. The Law has now become a guideline instead of a precondition.

Prayer

Thank You, Lord, for enabling me to have eternal life.

Today's Quote

For the wages of sin is death,
but the gift of God is eternal life in Christ Jesus our Lord.
— The Apostle Paul *(Romans 6: 23 NIV)*

It is all about faith, hope and love

Bible passage

Galatians 5 *Faith that shows*

5 But we expect to be made completely holy because of our *faith* in Christ. Through the Holy Spirit we wait in *hope*. [6] ... The only thing that really counts is faith that shows itself through *love*. *(NIrV)*

Devotion

To Paul, there were three words that described a Christian's life: faith, hope and love. He begins in Galatians 5 by talking about hope and expectation and then uses this to illustrate that Christians are geared toward the future. Hope is normally a reaction to uncertainty. When someone says I "hope" my team will win, he or she is not sure that it will indeed happen. But in the Bible the word "hope" is used completely differently. It expresses absolute certainty. Paul was absolutely certain that a believer did not have to fear the Day of Judgment, because he or she has already been acquitted on the ground of his or her faith.

In verse 6 Paul uses the words "faith" and "love" to emphasize that we as Christians are not only geared toward the future (hope), but are also people of action. Surely, we can't sit around idly waiting for Jesus to come. We have to keep ourselves busy in a meaningful way, and the only way to keep busy meaningfully is to live a life of faith. We can do this by performing good deeds. These deeds are not performed in a clinical and cold-hearted way, but with a heart filled with love. Faith never operates in isolation. True faith always becomes actions through love. It is therefore wrong to regard faith and deeds as separate entities. Paul saw them as a unity of believing and doing. Doing is not less important than believing.

Prayer

Lord, help me to show others what faith looks like by the way I live.

Today's Quote

Faith is the strength by which a shattered world shall emerge into the light.
—Helen Keller

Realizing that mathematically one cannot be three

Bible passage
Ephesians 1

17 I keep asking that the God of our Lord Jesus Christ, the glorious Father, may give you the Spirit of wisdom and revelation, so that you may know him better. *(NIV)*

Devotion

In the early third century, Tertullian, a prolific early Christian author from North Africa, coined the term Trinity and was the first author to talk about God as "three Persons, one Substance." "Person" comes from the Latin word "persona" which means a mask. In Roman theatres, one character could play different roles by wearing a mask. (Miley Cyrus wears a wig to become Hannah Montana)

The metaphor of God as the author of life (Acts 3: 15) will help us to better understand the concept of the Trinity. When an author writes a book, the author determines what the characters will say and how they will act. In the story of life, with God as the author, we are alive and subsequently we have the option of saying "yes," to the author of life or "no." Genesis 6 tells us that God was grieved by the choices of the characters. They wanted to write their own script and it lead to destruction. The best way for God the Father to talk to us is by writing Himself into the story. And so He does. God sends Jesus, who says to the disciples, if you have seen me you have seen the Father (Joh 14: 9).

After Jesus' ascension the Holy Spirit came to continually remind us, as characters, how to play our roles and how to play them correctly. In the story of life the same God plays three different roles.

Prayer
Thank you that You have revealed yourself to us in different ways.

Today's Quote
A religion without mystery must be a religion without God.
—Jeremy Taylor

So much truth in Leonard Cohen's quote

Bible passage

Ephesians 5 *Living in the Light*
9 The light produces what is completely good, right and true.
[13] But everything the light shines on can be seen. *(NIrV)*

Devotion

Many people shut up their heartache and secrets with a lock that says: "Nobody is allowed to hear about this." These locks should be unlocked. Why?

If we were to lock a dead animal away in one of the rooms in our house, the stench would gradually spread to the rest of the house and overpower us. In the same way, the shame and hurt that we lock away will eventually have a visible effect on our lives. We do not solve our problems by locking them away. On the contrary, they only get worse.

Paul called the key to unlock the locks of our inner rooms "light." This key of light helps us to see what we need to deal with. To open up our heart in prayer, or to someone we trust, gives us an opportunity to have remorse and to be forgiven. Things that keep on happening in the dark will spread insidiously. This is why women nowadays are urged to unlock the locks of molestation, rape and abuse and expose these deeds in order to hopefully bring an end to them.

So many people have told about the liberating feeling they experienced after they unlocked the hurt within them. So don't wait any longer to unlock your heartache. Dare to trust someone else to help you open the locks. This will be worth the trouble and pain!

Prayer
Lord, help me to unlock the locks of my pain.

Today's Quote
There is a crack in everything. That's how the light gets in.
—Leonard Cohen

My Son has been the greatest leader of all time

Bible passage

Philippians 1 *Paul's Life for Christ*

20 I honestly expect and hope that I will never do anything to be ashamed of. Whether I live or die, I always want to be as brave as I am now and bring honor to Christ. *(CEV)*

Devotion

What exactly makes someone a leader? Is it someone with a title or someone who occupies a high position? Should a leader be well spoken and knowledgeable? Moses was slow of speech but was a great leader despite this handicap. So what makes a true leader?

Mother Teresa was considered a leader because she influenced people all over the world. Princess Diana was a leader (although people seldom spoke about her in this way) because she had millions of followers all over the world.

Leadership is influence. People judge a leader by his or her followers. Hitler was considered a leader but the conduct of his followers and Hitler's approval of the actions of his followers made him a bad leader.

Paul realizes that a leader is measured in terms of his or her followers. That is why he said, "I honestly expect and hope that I will never do anything to be ashamed of." Our conduct is to Christ's honor or shame. Leadership is therefore not measured according to someone's position but according to the person's influence on others.

As a leader, Jesus' command makes sense, "If any of you wants to be my follower, you must turn from your selfish ways, take up your cross, and follow me" (Matt 16: 24). His honor is at stake!

Prayer

Lord, I pray that my life will bring glory and honor to You!

Today's Quote

Leadership is influence.

—John C. Maxwell

Not botox that will make the difference

Bible passage

Philippians 4: 4-5 *Joy*

4 Rejoice in the Lord always. I will say it again: Rejoice!
⁵ Let your gentleness be evident to all. *(TNIV)*

Devotion

It would be interesting to walk around and ask people, "What does a Christian look like?" I am sure that some of the answers would be embarrassing to us as Christians. Perhaps we should change the question somewhat. Let's rather ask, "What *should* a Christian look like?"

In this passage, Paul tells us very clearly what a Christian should look like: joyful and gentle! Both of these characteristics are based on choice. We therefore have no excuse not to have these two qualities. Both of them are also focused: Joy focuses on the Lord and gentleness focuses on all people.

Why does joy not focus on circumstances instead? Perhaps because then we would believe the lie that we could only be happy under favorable circumstances. Paul found himself in unsuitable circumstances - a prison - but urged the people to rejoice in the Lord.

The lesson Paul teaches us is that joy should not be dependent on circumstances. Paul was happy and joyous because he knew that Jesus Christ was with him in all circumstances. Therefore, his joy was in the Lord. This joy should flow over to all people in the form of gentleness, which means that we will act kindly toward all people. By doing this, we will captivate the world.

Prayer

Lord, I confess that I do not always live with joy and gentleness.

Today's Quote

If you would fall into any extreme, let it be on the side of gentleness. The human mind is so constructed that it resists rigor, and yields to softness.
—Saint Francis de Sales

Paul's signature words are the hope of glory

Bible passage

Colossians 1

27 To them God has chosen to make known … the glorious riches of this mystery, which is Christ in you, the hope of glory. *(NIV)*

Devotion

Christian Smith and Melinda Lundquist Denton (both sociologists) have coined a phrase that describes perfectly the dominant American religion: Moralistic Therapeutic Deism (MTD). After interviewing over 3,000 teenagers, the social scientists summed up their beliefs in the book: Soul Searching: The Religious and Spiritual Lives of American Teenagers:

1. "A god exists who created and ordered the world and watches over human life on earth."

2. "God wants people to be good, nice, and fair to each other, as taught in the Bible and by most world religions."

3. "The central goal of life is to be happy and to feel good about oneself."

4. "God does not need to be particularly involved in one's life except when God is needed to resolve a problem."

5. "Good people go to heaven when they die."

Christianity is about grace, not moralism. It's about changing lives, not making people feel better about themselves. It is about Christ in you.

How MTD's treat God reminds me of the title of the book "Get Out of My Life, But First Take Me and Alex into Town: A Parents Guide to the New Teenager." God is only good when you need Him. What "Just do it" is to Nike, "Christ in you" is to Paul. Christ in us is the hope of glory!

Prayer

Thank You, Lord that our hope is in You! To You be the glory!

Today's Quote

… because the one who is in you is greater than the one who is in the world.
— The Apostle John *(1 John 4: 4 NIV)*

Keep the main thing the main thing

Bible passage

Colossians 1

28 We proclaim him, admonishing and teaching everyone with all wisdom, so that we may present everyone perfect in Christ. *(NIV)*

Devotion

The apostle Paul proclaims Christ. That is the main thing! He did not proclaim clever human insights, life improvement, stress management, career enhancement, a system of beliefs, a set of traditions or superiority of church people over unchurched people.

In Colossian 1: 15-20 he explains why he proclaims Christ. Christ is the visible image of God. When you are in Christ (belonging to Christ) your life will be transformed in order to become mature in Christ. We cannot expect the world to believe the gospel of transformation from untransformed people. The world is in need of transformation and not more information.

Ruth Bell Graham, wife of international evangelist Billy Graham, shares the true account of a young college student from India, by the name of Pashi, who once told her, "I would like to believe in Christ. We of India would like to believe in Christ. But we have never seen a Christian who was like Christ." Ruth Graham says that when she consulted Dr. Akbar Haqq (former Muslim who converted to Christianity) about what might be the best response to Pashi's challenge, Haqq answered decisively, "That is quite simple. I would tell Pashi, 'I am not offering you Christians. I am offering you Christ.'"

Prayer

God, I thank You for Jesus, the One who is able to transform me.

Today's Quote

I like your Christ, I do not like your Christians. Your Christians are so unlike your Christ.
—Mahatma Gandhi

Paul is right! Be thankful in all circumstances

Bible passage

1 Thessalonians 5

18 give thanks in all circumstances, *(NIV)*

Devotion

The word "thank" and the word "think" are from the same root word, and this is no accident. The two words have much in common. Thankfulness grows out of thoughtfulness. Our focus on giving thanks improves our perspective.

Thanksgiving improves our perspective about ourselves. Alex Haley, the author of "Roots," had a picture of a turtle on top of a fence post hanging on his office wall. It reminded him that every time he wrote something significant and began to feel proud of himself, he looked at the turtle on top of the fence post and remembered that he didn't get there on his own. He had help.

Thanksgiving improves our perspective about our things. It causes us to count our blessings and to concentrate on what we do have.

Thanksgiving improves our perspective about God. Thanksgiving helps us to focus our attention on God's grace and power.

There was once a legend about a man who found the barn where Satan kept his seeds to be sown in the human heart. On finding the seeds of discouragement more numerous than the others, he learned that those seeds could grow almost anywhere. When Satan was questioned, he reluctantly admitted that there was one place he could never get them to thrive. "And where was that?" asked the man. Satan sadly replied, "In the heart of a grateful person."

Prayer

Lord, help me to be more grateful and thoughtful.

Today's Quote

Who does not thank for little will not thank for much.
—Estonian Proverb

A liberating request of only three words

Bible passage

2 Thessalonians 3: 1-5 *Paul's Request for Prayer*
1 Finally, our friends, please pray for us. *(CEV)*

Devotion

Life is not easy, and many people find life's challenges just too much to handle. Often times, people would rather just throw in the towel than persevere. Divorce, nervous breakdowns and suicides—to mention but a few—point to this fact. Paul, despite being a spiritual giant, also went through difficult times (2 Cor. 11:16-33). I must admit that after reading what Paul had to go through, I would have thrown in the towel a long time ago if I were in his shoes. But despite all of his hardships, Paul persevered. He could do so because he was prepared to make a very important request - one that we often neglect to make.

This spiritual giant was willing to ask the young congregation: "Pray for us" (v. 1). He made the same request in his other letters (1 Thess. 5:25; Philem. 22; Rom. 15:30). Paul realized that prayer helps you to persevere.

It is very liberating to pray for others and to ask others to pray for you. Imagine how your child would feel when he or she opened his or her lunchbox (just before a big test) and found a note with these words: "Mommy and Daddy love you and are praying for you!" Imagine a boy asking his friend to pray for him when he goes on his first date.

My uncle Jimmy, who passed away just before the completion of this devotion, often reminded me that he prayed every week for my family and me by name. I know that my mom still does. It is comforting and helps you to persevere!

Prayer

Thank You, Lord, for the privilege of praying for one another.

Today's Quote

Seven days without prayer makes one weak.
— Allen E. Vartlett

Don't fear criticism too much

Bible passage

1 Timothy 4: 12-16 *A Good Servant of Christ Jesus*
12 Don't let anyone make fun of you, just because you are young. Set an *example* for other followers by what you say and do, as well as by your love, faith, and purity. *(CEV)*

Devotion

As a young minister, Timothy had to prepare himself to handle criticism and opposition. The experienced Paul understood this and gave Timothy (and us) excellent advice on how to handle criticism.

According to Paul, there were two primary ways that Timothy should handle criticism. First, Timothy had to concentrate on setting a good *example*. Good arguments and polemics do not necessarily silence your critics. You might win the argument but lose the person in the process. The impact of your example is greater than the impact of your arguments. Example is better than precept.

A second way that Paul told Timothy to handle criticism was to stay focused on his mission: "Be sure to keep on reading the Scriptures in worship, and don't stop preaching and teaching" (v. 13). Criticism is usually aimed at the person and not the calling, so a good way to handle criticism is to divert the attention it brings away from yourself and remain fixed on your purpose. Paul knew that there was nothing as enriching as focusing on your mission, and nothing is as taxing as meddling in peripheral matters.

We have no control over what others say about us, but we do have control over the example we set and the calling on which we focus!

Prayer

Thank You, Lord, that I need not fear criticism.

Today's Quote

A good example has twice the value of good advice.
— Author unknown

Having a hard time talking about death?

Bible passage

2 Timothy 4

7 I have fought the good fight, I have *finished the race*, I have kept the faith. ⁸ Now there is in store for me the crown of righteousness, *(ESV)*

Devotion

An easy way to ruin a good party is to talk about death. As a rule, people don't like to talk about death. It reminds us of grief and loss. The big reason we avoid talking about death is the uncertainty about what will happen when you die, and that creates anxiety. Maybe Woody Allen's words captured many people's attitude towards death. He said: *"I'm not afraid to die, I just don't want to be there when it happens."*

Death casts a shadow over our lives on a daily basis. Nobody can escape it. We pretend that it doesn't exist and will never happen to us. The apostle Paul, however, was not afraid to talk about death. Paul lived with the conviction that our last enemy, death, had been conquered when Jesus died and rose from the dead (1 Cor 15: 26). Paul believed that in Christ all will be made alive (1 Cor 15: 22). Therefore, Paul saw his impending death as the *finish to a race* followed by a reward – eternal life. Paul lived with the conviction "For to me, to live is Christ and to die is gain" (Phil 1:22).

The following words by Jesus are so comforting: "Do not let your hearts be troubled. Trust in God; trust also in me. In my Father's house are many rooms; if it were not so, I would have told you. I am going there to prepare a place for you" (John 14: 1-2 *NIV*).

Prayer

Thank You, Lord, that death is a finishing line with a reward.

Today's Quote

I am the resurrection and the life.
He who believes in me will live, even though he dies.
—Jesus Christ *(John 11: 25 NIV)*

Well said, Paul

Bible passage

Titus 2

5 Each of the younger women must be sensible and kind, as well as a good homemaker, who puts her own husband first. Then no one can say insulting things about God's message. [8] Use clean language that no one can criticize. Do this, and your enemies will be too ashamed to say anything against you. *(CEV)*

Devotion

Is the Bible Still Credible? There are many different answers to this question. Arguments, no matter how good, will not easily convince opponents of the Word about its credibility. But there is something else that will embarrass the critics of God's Word.

Paul states that our exemplary conduct will make opponents of the Bible think twice before criticizing us (v. 8). An irreproachable life will confirm the virtuous, good and sound doctrines of the Bible. However, we should live out what we learn, for if we listen to the doctrines of God's grace and forgiveness but do not live accordingly, we discredit the Word of God (v. 4). Christians should excel in those things non-Christians also regard as virtuous—things such as honesty, fidelity, sincerity, punctuality and trustworthiness, to mention just a few.

Saint Francis of Assisi once said, "Preach the gospel at all times, and if necessary, use words." Test yourself: If you were accused of being a Christian, would there be enough evidence to prove that you are guilty? Martin Luther said that you should live in such a way that even your dog would know that you are a Christian.

Prayer
Lord, I want to commit myself anew to live according to Your will.

Today's Quote
Few things are harder to put up with than the annoyance of a good example.
—Mark Twain

So glad the way Paul treated the runaway slave

Bible passage

Philemon *Paul's Plea for Onesimus*

10 I beg you to help Onesimus! He is like a son to me because I led him to Christ here in jail. *(CEV)*

Devotion

The short letter of Philemon, which consists of 25 verses that Paul wrote from prison to his friend Philemon in Colosse around AD 60, contains a very important message for us. It requires us to break down the walls in our churches (and society)—not the concrete walls, but the barriers of race, sexism, social status, gender and personality differences that so often exist. The two characters in the letter, namely Philemon and Onesimus, are striking examples of such barriers.

Philemon was the master, and Onesimus the slave. The separation between them grew when Onesimus ran away. However, this runaway slave's path crossed with that of Paul, and their meeting led to Onesimus's conversion. Paul sent Onesimus, the slave, back to Philemon with a letter addressed to his master.

In those days, slavery was a common practice, and it is clear from Paul's letter that Christians also participated in the practice. Paul never openly criticized slavery, but in this letter he dealt the barrier a devastating blow. How did he do this? He asked Philemon to take back his slave, Onesimus, as a brother in Christ. He told Philemon that their relationship had changed from that of a master and slave to one between fellow believers. In Christ, all of us belong to one big family. No barriers should bring discord between believers.

Prayer

Lord, I want to break down the barriers that exist in my life!

Today's Quote

Do the right thing. It will gratify some people and astonish the rest.
—Mark Twain

barriers

Jesus Christ – liar, lunatic or Lord?

Bible passage

Hebrews 1

8 But he says to the Son,
You're God, and on the throne for good;
your rule makes everything right.
You love it when things are right; *(MSG)*

Devotion

Was Jesus Christ really the Son of God or was He just a good moral teacher? C. S. Lewis, who was a professor at Cambridge University and once an agnostic, understood this issue clearly. In his famous book Mere Christianity he makes it very clear that you must make your choice. Either this man was, and is, the Son of God: or else a madman or something worse. He said: *"You can shut Him up for a fool, you can spit at Him and kill Him as a demon; or you can fall at His feet and call Him Lord and God. But let us not come up with any patronizing nonsense about His being a great human teacher. He has not left that open to us. He did not intend to."*

If you believe Jesus was only a good moral teacher, what do you do with His claims that was such an integral part of his teachings?
Here are some of Jesus' claims:

▶ Jesus Christ claimed to live a sinless life (John 8:46-47)
▶ Jesus Christ claimed to be the only way to God (John 14:6)
▶ Jesus Christ claimed to be able to forgive sins (Luke 5:20-21)
▶ Jesus Christ claimed to be the Messiah (John 4: 25-26)

You have one of three choices. He was as a Liar, Lunatic or Lord.
Another way to put it is that He was Mad, Bad, or God.

Prayer

Jesus, I have made my choice. You are Lord!

Today's Quote

I am the way and the truth and the life.
—Jesus Christ *(John 14: 6 NIV).*

Wondering where I was on September 11, 2001?

Bible passage

Hebrews 4: 14-16 *God feels our reality*

15 We don't have a priest who is out of touch with our reality. He's been
through weakness and testing, experienced it all - all but the sin. *(MSG)*

Devotion

The world, especially America, will never be the same again after
September 11, 2001. When people think about the tragic events that
occurred on that day, they often ask each other, "Where were you when
it happened?" But there is a much more difficult question that is also
often asked, namely: "Where was God when it happened?"

The following story illustrates something that we cannot accuse God of
doing. During the 1930s, a father found his daughter crying next to the
radio in her room. When he asked her why she was so sad, she told him
that she had heard a news report over the radio that said Japanese tanks
had invaded Canton that day. This had very little significance for most of
the people who listened to the news that day. So why was the girl in tears?
It was because she was born in Canton. To her, Canton meant a loving
home, school and friends. She could say, "I was there!"

For each human experience, God can also say, "I was there!" Through
Jesus, God became a human being so that He could experience every
possible human experience (v. 15).

Prayer

Thank You, Lord, that I know that You are not distant and cold.

Today's Quote

*The flood that devastates a town is not an "act of God," even if the insurance
companies find it useful to call it that. But the efforts people make to save lives,
risking their own lives for a person who might be a total stranger to
them, and the determination to rebuild their community after the flood waters
have receded, do qualify as acts of God.*
— Harold Kushner

i was there

My Son was the perfect High Priest

Bible passage

Hebrews 7: 24-28 Jesus the perfect High Priest
26 So now we have a high priest who perfectly fits our needs: completely holy, uncompromised by sin, with authority extending as high as God's presence in heaven itself. *(MSG)*

Devotion

Why does religion exist? Religion exists because human beings have an inherent need for a deity. Religion provides access to such a deity. Christians believe that only Jesus can provide access to God. Why?

The Jewish religion was designed to bring human beings closer to God. This would be achieved in two ways: First, by establishing obedience to the Law, which brought a person closer to God; and second, through the introduction of the sacrificial system, which was necessary because it was impossible to achieve this kind of obedience to the Law. The priests' function was to open a way to God by means of this system. However, the system as a whole was ineffective because it failed to establish true peace between God and human beings. The offerings could not pay the price for sin, and the priests themselves had weaknesses (v. 28). The answer to this problem rested in another high priest and another offering.

In order to open a way to God, a high priest had to be fully in touch with human beings and with God. He had to know human beings and God perfectly. Only one person on earth claimed to be fully human and fully God: Jesus. Through Jesus we have access to God!

Prayer

Thank You, Lord, that Your sacrificial death opened the way to God for me.

Today's Quote

Jesus does not give recipes that show the way to God as other teachers of religion do. He is himself the way.
—Karl Barth

Fascinated with Larry King's interview with Joni

Bible passage

James 1: 1-4 *Faith and Endurance*
2 Consider it a sheer gift, friends, when tests and challenges come at you from all sides. *(MSG)*

Devotion

From time to time, we all find ourselves in a situation (often because of our own doing) from which we would like to escape. No one is immune to affliction and suffering, and it can make us extremely bitter. But the author of James asks us to change our attitude toward suffering. The tone of James' opening words to the believers who fled from Jerusalem is not gloomy. On the contrary, he asks them to consider their suffering as a gift. One is tempted to tell James that he is out of his mind to ask them to be happy when bitterness would be the logical emotion. However, James then explains in striking terms why they should rather see it as a gift. Suffering is a religious exercise.

Faith is precious, and in order for us to be strengthened against dejection and bitterness, we should exercise our faith. Trials do not exist to make us weaker and bitter but to make us stronger and better.

On August 3, 2004, I tuned in to Larry King Live to see an interview that he was conducting with Joni Eareckson Tada. Joni had become a quadriplegic in 1967 after a diving accident. While in a wheelchair, she wrote bestsellers and received many tributes and awards. When asked about her life in a wheelchair, she answered with a smile, "Larry, this wheelchair is my freedom. This wheelchair was instrumental in bringing me to Christ." She wasn't bitter but better—a symbol of hope!

Prayer

Thank You, Lord, that suffering helps me to be a better person!

Today's Quote

What seems to us as bitter trials are often blessings in disguise.
—Oscar Wilde

What Do Our Tongues and a Tube of Toothpaste Have in Common?

Bible passage

James 3: 1-5 *Controlling the Tongue*
3 A bit in the mouth of a horse controls the whole horse.
[4] A small rudder on a huge ship in the hands of a skilled captain sets a course in the face of the strongest winds. [5] A word out of your mouth may seem of no account, but it can accomplish nearly anything--or destroy it! *(MSG)*

Devotion

It has been said that the tongue is one of the most exercised muscles of our body. It has been estimated that in a typical week, the average person will speak enough words to fill a 500-page book! However, for the Christian, the use of the tongue must be a matter of careful forethought and discipline. There are times when we reproach ourselves for saying the wrong thing or we think we should have kept quiet instead.

It might help to realize that the tongue and a tube of toothpaste have something in common: once their contents are out, it cannot be put back. Therefore, we need to take extra caution before we say anything.

James says that the tongue performs the same work as the bit of a bridle or the rudder of a ship. In the same way that the bit and the rudder control something large, the tongue has the ability to control major things in our lives. In reality, we often stumble. We have two ears and one tongue and need to use them in the same ratio.

Prayer

Lord, help me to be careful how I use my tongue.

Today's Quote

Speaking without thinking is shooting without taking aim.
— Author unknown

Liking Peter's insights on perseverance

Bible passage

1 Peter 1

1 I, Peter, am an apostle on assignment by Jesus, the Messiah, writing to *exiles* scattered to the four winds. Not one is missing, not one forgotten. *(MSG)*

1 Peter 2 *This world is not your home*

11 Friends, this world is not your home, so don't make yourselves cozy in it. Don't indulge your ego at the expense of your soul. *(MSG)*

Devotion

In about AD 65, Peter wrote his first letter to the devastated believers in Asia Minor who were suffering greatly because society had rejected them. Peter wanted to give them hope to carry on with their lives. He did this by showing them how they had to see themselves in the world.

Peter feels strongly that believers should regard themselves as strangers in this world. It is why the two main sections of the book start with this thought. Before telling them anything else, Peter wanted them to understand that they were strangers in this world. But why would Peter want believers to regard themselves as strangers?

By regarding ourselves as strangers, many things become clear to us. The criticism, insults and suffering we experience as a Christian are precisely because our values and approach to life make us different from the rest of the world.

For the world it is about money, sex and power. For Christians, life is rather about faith, love and hope.

Prayer

Thank You, Lord, that I can see everything in perspective.

Today's Quote

The road to success is dotted with many tempting parking places.

— Author Unknown

strangers

Waiting not as bad as you think

Bible passage

2 Peter 3: 8-15 *God is never late*

8 Don't overlook the obvious here, friends. With God, one day is as good as a thousand years, a thousand years as a day. ⁹ God isn't late with his promise as some measure lateness. He is restraining himself on account of you, holding back the End because he doesn't want anyone lost. *(MSG)*

Devotion

One of the important instructions of the Bible is the call to "wait on the Lord." The reality is that we don't like to wait? We live in a society of instant gratification. Just think of fast food, the fast lane, express mail and high speed internet. But the reality of our day of conveniences, waiting is still a big part of life. We stand in lines, wait for a job interview and sit in the traffic.

After waiting for almost 40 years for Jesus to return, the second generation of Christians, to whom Peter wrote his second letter, was very tired of waiting. We have been waiting 2,000 years for Jesus to return, and many of us might be wondering whether He has forgotten about us. Will Jesus really return? God has not forgotten us. Peter gives two reasons why God is still waiting to send Jesus back to earth. First, Peter reminds us that time is not the same for us as it is for God (v 8). God lives in eternity. For this reason, human beings cannot calculate when the second coming will occur.

Second, Peter calls this time of waiting a time of grace. What we consider waiting is actually an expression of God's patience with us. God wants to give people the opportunity to be saved.

Prayer

Thank You, Lord, for Your grace and Your great patience with me!

Today's Quote

Patience comes to those who wait.
—Terry Ballard

Eternity a reality that can be yours

Bible passage

1 John 5 *Eternal life*

10 Whoever *believes* in the Son of God inwardly confirms God's testimony. Whoever refuses to *believe* in effect calls God a liar, refusing to *believe* God's own testimony regarding his Son. [11] This is the testimony in essence: God gave us eternal life; the life is in his Son. [12] So, whoever has the Son, has life; whoever rejects the Son, rejects life. *(MSG)*

Devotion

How would you define eternity? A mother who has to wait 40 seconds for a bottle to heat up while her baby is crying in the background might feel that these seconds are an eternity. For some, the last minutes of a game can feel like an eternity.

During the fifth century, Augustine, the great church father, said that time only exists within creation. God exists outside of time. He does not have a past or a future, only an eternal now. Eternal life is therefore nothing else but God's life. The good news is that we can be part of this eternal life and that we can be certain about it. But how?

The following analogy may help to clarify this idea. If we want to meet someone who moves outside our circle of friends, the best course of action would be for us to find someone who knows the person and who is willing to introduce us to him or her. This is what Jesus achieved for us with regard to God. Jesus knows the Father fully and gives us access to the Him.

Prayer

Lord, it amazes me to know I have eternal life.

Today's Quote

Life: a front door to eternity.

— Author unknown

John Lennon was right when he sang: "All you need is love"

Bible passage

2 John *Live in Truth*

1 My dear congregation, I, your pastor, *love* you in very truth. And I'm not alone - everyone who knows the Truth [2]that has taken up permanent residence in us loves you. [3] Let grace, mercy, and peace be with us in truth and *love* from God the Father and from Jesus Christ, Son of the Father! (MSG)

Devotion

In the letter of 2 John, which consist of only 245 words, John delivers a short but powerful message. He wrote the letter around AD 95, possibly from a mother church (the recipients of 1 John) to a sister church (the recipients of 2 John) to point out the two fundamental principles of the Christian faith to them. These principles would protect them against the false doctrines of heretics. Even today, we are all still looking for these two principles, but unfortunately they are so difficult to find.

John refers to the two principles of truth and love. Truth and love are inseparably linked in all of John's letters. These two principles give meaning to life. The Beatles were right in 1967 when they sang "All You Need Is Love." The only way to experience love is to value truth as well.

Even today, people in a court of law have to take an oath to ensure that they speak the truth. Think about it: one cannot build healthy relationships and experience true love without truth. How many scars have been caused because of lies?

Prayer

Lord, today I want to start, anew, to show *agape* love toward others.

Today's Quote

The whole being of any Christian is faith and love. Faith brings the man to God; love brings him to men.

—Martin Luther

Putting my love in action

Bible passage

3 John: 1-8 *Caring for the Lord's Workers*

1 The Pastor, to my good friend Gaius: How truly I love you! ² We're the best of friends, and I pray for good fortune in everything you do, and for your good health - that your everyday affairs prosper, as well as your soul! ⁵ Dear friend, when you extend hospitality to Christian brothers and sisters, even when they are strangers, you make the faith visible. *(MSG)*

Devotion

This short letter, consisting of only a few words, differs from the first two letters because it is addressed to a person and not a congregation. In this letter, John asks his friend Gaius to show something specific toward the traveling preachers: hospitality. Hospitality causes no one any harm; in fact, it makes people feel very special.

Hospitality is derived from the Latin word *"hosped"*. It is interesting that both the words guest and host are derived from the same Latin word. In modern English, we think of the two words as antonyms. This is not the paradox that one might think: a host cannot be a host without a guest, and it is impossible to be a guest without a host.

"Hospitality" can also mean generously providing care and kindness to whoever is in need. The word hospital comes to mind and it is also derived from the same Latin word *"hosped"*.

Hospitality allows people to feel comfortable and at home because hospitality is God's love in action. Hospitality enables people to experience God's love.

Prayer

Thank You, Lord, that I can use hospitality to make Your love visible.

Today's Quote

Who practices hospitality entertains God Himself.
—Unknown

Not to gamble with this

Bible passage

Jude *The Danger of False Teachers*

4 What has happened is that some people have infiltrated our ranks (our Scriptures warned us this would happen), who beneath their pious skin are shameless scoundrels. *Their design is to replace the sheer grace of our God with sheer license* – which means doing away with Jesus Christ, our one and only Master. *(MSG)*

Devotion

The author of the letter/sermon of Jude was most likely the brother of James and Jesus. The letter was probably written sometime between AD 60 and 70. It is not clear to whom the letter was written, but it would appear as if the author knew the believers to whom it was directed. It is clear that the tone of his letter is personal, serious and urgent. The urgency of the letter was fuelled by a dangerous gamble in the congregation.

He wanted to urgently warn the congregation against individuals who had secretly infiltrated the congregation and were leading them to gamble with God's grace. These individuals believed that God's grace provided them with a free ticket to immorality, as they were under the impression that God's grace was encompassing enough to compensate for their immoral life.

These individuals' view was that people should sin bravely because they know that the grace of God is great. They abused God's grace to justify their immoral lifestyle. They saw God's grace as an invitation to be sinful. Yet, no one should gamble with God's grace.

Prayer

Lord, forgive me if I have gambled with your grace.

Today's Quote

Grace isn't a little prayer you chant before receiving a meal. It's a way to live.
— Jackie Windspear

Do You Think Evil Triumphs—I Have News For You!

Bible passage

Revelation 5 *The Lamb Opens the Scroll*

6 So I looked, and there, surrounded by Throne, Animals, and Elders, was a Lamb, slaughtered but standing tall. Seven horns he had, and seven eyes, the Seven Spirits of God sent into all the earth. *(MSG)*

Devotion

The recipients of the book of Revelation were Christians who were persecuted terribly. In such trying times, one may feel like throwing in the towel because it seems as if evil triumphs. Today, it still seems as if the Church has lost its impact on society. Yet in such times, the book of Revelation brings us hope.

John had a poignant vision of God. In this vision Jesus is the Lion as well as the Lamb. How is this possible? One is a hunter, while the other is the prey. God allowed Jesus to become the prey of our sins. In this way, He conquered death not with the power of a lion but with the love of the Lamb's blood.

On October 30, 1974, Mohammad Ali and George Foreman fought against each other in Zaire (now the Democratic Republic of the Congo). Ali held his hands in front of his face, leaned against the ropes and allowed Foreman, the overwhelming favorite, to have a go at him for eight rounds. When the right moment came, Ali bounced off the ropes and knocked out Foremen, sending him into retirement. Ali called his technique "rope-a-dope." Even though it looked as if he was losing the fight—and losing badly—he was in control the whole time. In the same way, God is in control—even if this does not always seem to be the case.

Prayer

Thank You, Lord, that I know that You are in control.

Today's Quote

Anything under God's control is never out of control.
—Charles Swindoll

Be aware of this strategy of evil

Bible passage

Revelation 17 *The Great Prostitute*

5 A mysterious name was written on her forehead: "Babylon the Great, Mother of All Prostitutes and Obscenities in the World." *(NLT)*

Devotion

In John's time, one could sum up Roman culture in three words: money, sex and power! In this section, the immoral and materialistic lifestyle of Roman culture is presented as a prostitute. The prostitute is presented as Babylon (v. 5), a symbolic name for Rome because Rome, like Babylon of old, threatened the existence of God's new people, the Christians. Rome is also called Babylon because, like that nation, Rome destroyed the Temple in Jerusalem.

John was carried away in a vision to look at the woman in the desert. This was in the same spot where the Church was (Rev. 12:6), which shows that the Church was not immune to the influence of this infamous woman.

It is sad to see how many Christians have stumbled before the temptations of money, sex and power. This section in Revelation makes it clear that the culture in which we live can exert an enormous influence over our lives. As Christians, we must be aware of the temptations of money, sex and power. We must be honest and admit that it is not always easy to resist them! Materialism and immorality lead to an addiction to gambling, illicit sex and pornography and eventually causes our downfall. If you are caught up in this evil grip, it would be wise to talk about it with someone whom you trust. It will not disappear spontaneously. Victory is possible!

Prayer

Lord, please protect me from the dangers of money, sex and power.

Today's Quote

Temptation is a woman's weapon and man's excuse.
—Henry Louis Mencken

From a Garden to a City

Bible passage

Revelation 22

20 He who testifies to all these things says it again:
'I'm on my way! I'll be there soon!' Yes! Come, Master Jesus!
21 The grace of the Master Jesus be with all of you. Oh, Yes! *(MSG)*

Devotion

If Genesis describes the beginning of God's history with human beings, the book of Revelation describes its conclusion. The very first verse in the Bible begins with God: "In the beginning God created the heavens and the earth." (Gen 1:1, *NIV*). The very last verse of the Bible also ends with God: "The grace of the Master Jesus be with all of you. Oh, Yes!" (Rev. 22:21). One could put this differently: the Bible starts with paradise and ends with paradise. But there is one big difference—in Revelation, evil is destroyed forever.

Genesis tells us about a garden of paradise with an evil snake, while the book of Revelation sketches a picture of a perfect city without evil. Sin destroyed the Garden of Eden for us, but the spiritual paradise is created anew in the New Jerusalem (Rev. 21). Our journey through the Bible takes place between these two paradises.

What does this mean to me today while I'm struggling with all my pain, trying to keep my head above water amidst all the chaos in the world? Revelation wants to encourage us by saying that: The world is not heading towards an aimless end, but to an endless hope in God's company.

Prayer
Thank You, Lord, that You embrace me with Your grace!

Today's Quote
I haven't a clue as to how my story will end. But that's all right. When you set out on a journey and night covers the road, you don't conclude the road has vanished. And how else could we discover the stars?
— Author unknown